The Deaf/Blind Baby
A programme of care

The author and Bunty when she was two.

The Deaf/Blind Baby

A programme of care

Peggy Freeman M.B.E.

Illustrations by Pat Kay

William Heinemann Medical Books
London

To Bunty, Nana and Mandy who were the inspiration for this programme.

First published 1985
by William Heinemann Medical Books Ltd
23 Bedford Square, London WC1B 3HH

ISBN 0–433–10906–8

Typeset by Wilmaset
Birkenhead, Merseyside

Printed in Great Britain by Spottiswoode Ballantyne,
Colchester, Essex

Contents

Introduction

In 1973 I wrote a booklet called *A Parent's Guide to the Early Care of a Deaf/Blind Child*. It was described as part 1 of a series, and I had planned to write three further booklets. However, pressure to produce the rest of the series resulted in the whole (including Part 1) being published in 1975 under the title *Understanding the Deaf/Blind Child*.

It is now 1984, and in the intervening years I have continued to have close contact with very young deaf/blind children and their parents, particularly in the context of the Parent/Baby Weekend Courses and the Preschool Teaching Unit at the National Association's Family Centre in London. I have also been privileged to visit many overseas centres where exciting work is going on for this age group. All this has led me, I believe, to a better understanding of the needs of the very young deaf/blind child, and this present programme aims to share this with his parents.

This book, therefore, is an enlargement of the original part 1 booklet, and the 1975 book remains valid for the older age group. Chapter 1 is concerned with some of the things parents need to know—I hope it contains some answers to some of the questions parents should ask, but rarely do. We cannot fulfil our role as parents active in the education of our disabled children unless we understand their problems and needs and are aware of the resources to help us—Chapters 2 and 3 cover these aspects. We take for granted our use of vision and hearing, for we do not remember a time when we were not seeing or listening, or a time when we had no words and could not communicate with others. We need therefore to be reminded of the functions of vision and hearing and how visual and auditory skills develop, so that we can help the deaf/blind child to use what he possesses despite the impairments—so Chapter 4 is devoted to this.

The programme then follows, and is set out under three headings:

The experience(s) the deaf/blind baby needs to have
What you can do to provide these experiences
Why this is necessary (except where this would merely be repetition).

The programme is divided into six stages and these have no age reference—progress is continuous and so long as it *is* continuing, the child must be allowed to go at his own rate and not be compared with the child who has full use of his vision and hearing. Each stage is preceded by some general comments. Finally, there are four samples of individually planned programmes, a schedule of normal child development to remind you of the milestones, a list of books and toys, and a few other items including the Finger Spelling Chart which I hope will be useful.

This programme is intended for parents, but should also provide some insight for others who share the care and education of deaf/blind children. It may not be without its critics. Although the normal developmental sequence has been followed, it has been spread over a longer period and I have made some adjustments to take account of the differences I have observed in deaf/blind children. These should also allow for the developmental delay consequent upon the lack of full vision and hearing and the slower acquisition of knowledge through the sense of touch and a less easily learned method of communication. No two deaf/blind children are alike, so while it fits one child in some areas, it may not fit another. But I am confident that, if I have succeeded in identifying the crucial areas and the special techniques needed and have shown how small steps are necessary to build up skills, parents will themselves be able to make any adjustments that may be necessary. Fraiberg (1977) said of parents that their intervention in a programme was its most important aspect: 'if they could overcome the natural anxiety and stress associated with having a disabled child, they would be able to develop the normal love-bonds and affectionate care'. This is undoubtedly true, but by itself not enough. Parents need the information that enables them to understand their child's needs and necessitates the special approach, if they are to be able to carry out the programme successfully. This has been evident to me in the many encounters I have had over the years with parents of deaf/blind children and is the reason for the form in which this book has been written.

I would like to express my thanks to the parents and teachers who have so willingly shared their special knowledge with me, some of whom have been kind enough to read and comment on the script during the preparation of the programme. My thanks also to my husband Peter for his help while I have been writing this book and for his support during the nearly 30 years that we have together been working for deaf/blind children. Also to Sarah Green for typing most of the manuscripts and Mrs Pat Kay for the line drawings. And special thanks to all those young disabled children with whom it has been my joy to work and play.

Peggy Freeman

1 *First thoughts*

When a disabled child is born, his parents are faced with an experience they could not have foreseen and for which they are neither ready nor prepared. We need a little time to sort out our thoughts, but we also urgently need information and reassurance. We worry about the future; how will we cope, what will people say and what will our child be like as he grows up? Psychologists say that following the birth of a disabled child, parents go through a number of identifiable emotional stages as they come to terms with this new situation which may affect their hopes, ambitions and lifestyle. Perhaps we do, subconsciously and some of the time, but I am certain most of us would recover our equilibrium more quickly if, early on, we could have contact with someone who has gone through the same experience, someone who can assure us that it is never as bad as we imagine, that we do find the strength to cope when it is needed, that what others say depends very much on the way *we* view our child, and that the child will be himself, the same as any other child.

It is right to feel devastated and to cry a bit, feel anger, self pity—we are human and these feelings are quite natural. It helps if you can talk to someone who knows and understands and who can tell you from experience that although there may be frustration, doubts, sorrow, aloneness, even failure in the coming months and years, there will be moments of intense joy, wonder and fulfilment as you meet a challenge with spirit and success.

As for our disabled child: we tend at first to think more about what we *imagine* he will *not* be able to do than what may well be within his ability—he will usually do a lot more than any of us expect. But this does depend largely upon you. No matter how many other people help your child along life's way (and there will be many), none will have a more lasting effect on him than you, his parents and his family.

At no time is this more important than during the first three years. This is the period when *all* children are acquiring those skills which they will later use to learn for themselves and which enable them to make relationships with other people and become social beings. Babies can see when they are born, but they take a while to learn to recognise what they see, a a bit longer to notice the difference between people and between objects so that each

1

has its own identity. Although children can hear at birth (and even before, it is believed), they have to learn to recognise and attach meaning to the words they hear and to learn how to make these sounds themselves, before they are able to communicate with us by speaking. (This takes two to three years.) When a child is born he has spontaneous reflex movements and he only gradually learns to control the movements he makes so that he can become mobile and get himself around and do things for and by himself. When a child is born he has no knowledge of himself as a person and others as separate from him—it is through the early interaction with his mother that he learns how to make relationships and, as he relates to other members of his family and beyond, learns to control his feelings and conform to the mores of the society in which he lives. Only when a child acquires these early learning and social skills can he begin to function as the independent, thinking little person in his own right that we recognise in most 5 year olds.

For the child who has an impairment in both vision and hearing from birth, learning these skills is a necessity just as for any other child. It is quite rare for the impairment in both to be total, so making sure a child makes the best possible use of his *residual* (remaining) vision and hearing is absolutely vital to the development of the early learning and social skills. It is not the

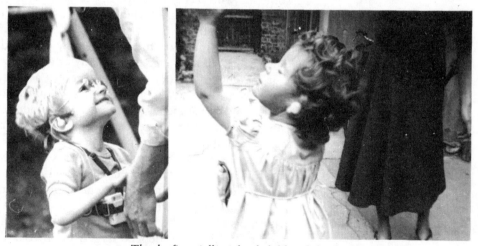

The deaf/partially sighted child and the deaf/blind child.

amount of vision and hearing he has that matters so much as that he *uses* it well, and that it 'handicaps' him as little as possible. There is a distinction between the words 'disability' and 'handicap' which we should bear in mind here. *Disability* describes the impairment, i.e. the deafness and blindness, *handicap* is the restriction placed by the disability upon the child's ability to function normally. While the deaf/blind child has disabilities, he also has *abilities* which may include some useful vision and/or hearing. Until he has had an opportunity to learn to

2

use these, we do not know to what extent he *will be handicapped* by the disabilities; we must not anticipate the extent of this. Recognising the difference between these two terms also reminds us that we must concentrate on what the child has, rather than trying to make up for the loss. In the past many deaf/blind children were diagnosed as mentally handicapped before they had been given an opportunity to develop the early learning skills and show the areas in which they had abilities. They were treated as being ineducable; they fulfilled expectations and as a result did not develop intellectually. This can still happen.

Because there can be so many different combinations of deafness, and degrees of sight loss, it has always been difficult to define what we mean by the terms 'deaf/blind'. Generally, wherever there is the dual disability from birth, all such children will need the special kind of treatment which is suggested in this book to begin with. However, if, with early training, a child can learn to use his vision well enough to allow him to communicate visually (to lipread or see manual signs), it is more likely that he can be educated as a deaf child. If, with early training, he can learn to hear well enough to allow him to communicate with speech, it is more likely he can be educated as a visually impaired or blind child. If, however, the child has a combination of the two impairments and, despite early training, it is impossible for him to obtain sufficient information from the environment to enable him to make sense of his world without help, then he is a child who will need specialist deaf/blind education when he reaches school age.

So, early learning skills and the training of residual vision and hearing are prime aspects of helping your child, whatever the degree of visual and auditory loss. It is also very important that you have a very positive attitude to him. He has the same need as all of us to be loved, to share, to learn and grow. He needs your care but not overprotection, otherwise you will deny him the opportunity to explore, to try to do things for himself when he is ready, and to make choices for himself. Even if sometimes the result is negative, it can be of value, for to become a person he has to learn what it is to fail sometimes as well as succeed, to know unhappiness as well as joy. He has to grow up, change and, most of all, be himself like the rest of us—though with these children it is tempting to us as parents to keep them as 'children'.

Also, first and foremost, your disabled child is a member of the family. It is almost impossible to divide your time equally amongst the children in a family when one is less able than the others, and there is inevitably more to be done within the daily caring activities, but do take time out to have fun with all the family. When the time is ripe the disabled member must do his bit and help others—this is part of his independence. Because we think we would be helpless if we could not see and hear (since we are so used to having these skills), we tend to think that it is inevitable that the deaf/blind child will be helpless and so we rush to assist him and set this pattern within the family—we can so easily deny him the chance to learn to do for himself. Finding solutions to our own problems contributes to our personal growth and independence, and this is no less true of the disabled. Every time we can allow a deaf/blind child to figure out his own solution to his problem, he learns a new behaviour pattern to use in the future in a similar set of circumstances. Every time we deprive him of this opportunity, he learns to rely on us and learns nothing new. Every time we pull up his pants for him without showing him how to do it for himself, we are lessening the likelihood that he will learn to dress himself.

Only as his life unfolds and he shows you what he can do will you realise how great are your child's possibilities. So keep an open mind on how much he will be handicapped by his disabilities, do not limit him by the way you *think* of him or *describe* him to others. He will have his own contribution to make to the society of which he is part, particularly if he has a good start and the right kind of education to promote his intellectual growth.

Of course you will not be alone in helping your child to develop his potential. There will be people from various professions sharing the task with you. You will need their help and must never be afraid to ask for it. They will help you, but they will be better able to do this if you help them. You know your child better than any professional person can, for you live with him 24 hours of every day, 7 days a week, all 52 weeks of every year. You, his parents, are the experts on your child, and today professionals are much more aware of this than they used to be and much more willing to listen to what you have to contribute. So make sure you express your thoughts, observations and wishes for your child at all times, for these are basic to planning his education and training at every stage of his life.

People who work in the field of disability have chosen to do this and they can withdraw at any time they wish (although they rarely do, bless them); you did not choose to have a disabled child, and the responsibility for his care and seeing that his rights are upheld (until such time as he can do this for himself) is yours just as it would be if he were not disabled—we parents cannot opt out. In the past some of our duties and rights as parents have been handed over to professionals because we did not know enough to understand our role and its importance in the life of a disabled child. Thank goodness some of the old-fashioned attitudes are disappearing and parents are today regarded as educators of their children, with a right to the information that allows them to undertake the task properly.

Doctors and paediatricians are obviously the first to be concerned with our child, and we rely on them for information about the extent of his disabilities. Sometimes these conditions change: hearing can deteriorate, the state of the eye can alter. Regular checks by ophthalmologists and audiologists are essential to provide information for planning and carrying out suitable programmes. However, since there is no way of determining how well a child will use his residual vision and hearing until we see how he responds to the experiences we offer him, we should be wary of accepting as final any prognosis that might be offered—only time will tell and hope is *our* lifeline. Doctors will look to you for information, and everything you tell them will help to make their diagnosis more accurate, help them to determine which aids the child needs (glasses or hearing aid etc.) and to keep a check on his general health—a child who is not fit finds it much more difficult to learn.

Teachers are very important people in the preschool and school years of your child's life. They bridge the gap between home and the world. They know about *children*, they know the skills children need and the sequence along which their growth (physical and intellectual) should develop. They know how to build each new stage upon the structure of the previous one, and they have a wide range of special techniques with which to meet the needs of disabled children. You as parents could not do the best for your child without their help—teachers cannot use to best advantage their knowledge and skills unless you share with them your special understanding of your child. There must be a real partnership in planning both the aims and contents of the educational programme so that there is continuity in both situations.

From time to time your child will be 'assessed', probably by a team which will include doctors, psychologists, teachers, physiotherapists and others, the main purpose being to determine the level of development your child has achieved and to *recommend* future treatment, educational placement etc. The most important members of such a team are the parents. If this right to be part of the team or make decisions is denied you, then you must take action appropriate to your particular circumstances—do not accept what you feel is not right for your child without taking the matter further. Under the 1981 Education Act, the laws relating to the education of handicapped children have recently changed. From April 1983, individual categories were abolished and replaced by defining children with special needs as having learning difficulties.

Local education authorities (LEAs) have a duty to place children with special needs in ordinary schools, and special educational needs are to be met by support services in these schools. The Act requires LEAs to ensure that schools make special provision for all children who experience difficulties in their education. If a local health authority considers a child under 5 years old is in need of special educational treatment, the parents must be told and it must be brought to the notice of the LEA.

Names and addresses of relevant voluntary organisations that may be able to help them must also be given to parents. The needs of children with severe learning difficulties will be safeguarded by a new 'Statement of Needs' describing these and how they will be met.

There is to be greater involvement of parents in the assessment and placement of their children. They will contribute to the Statement with written representations. All information provided to LEAs to help them make decisions must be made available to parents as part of the Statement. Under the Law, parents will receive a copy of the Statement which will include education, medical, psychological and other reports. Discussions between parents and professionals during assessment will be of 'crucial importance'. The LEAs must also make arrangements for parents to appeal against the special educational provision written down in the Statement, and there is a further right of appeal to the Secretary of State. Do make certain that you are familiar with the rights of your child as a handicapped person and your rights as his parents.

Society can often be very cruel and the attitude of others more damaging to the feelings and lifestyle of the disabled child and his family than the actual disability itself. As a group, the disabled are still discriminated against by society—although the present trend to integrate them into the community should help to lessen this and bring about a greater understanding of the contribution they have to make. If once this could be said to be due to superstition passed down from person to person, today's knowledge and publicity leave no room for excuses now. Counselling exists, but there remains a great need to provide parents with additional pairs of hands to share in meeting the constant demands made on them during the child's preschool years. At present there is still a lack of co-ordination and direction in the specialist education without which no deaf/blind child can be expected to achieve his potential; there is still no adequate preparation for the move from school out into the world and no effort to provide occupational and community living for the deaf/blind in Britain. It is to be hoped that by the time your child has reached this stage, there will have been major changes in these areas in this country; if not, you too must join the fight begun by parents like myself long ago to see that these rights are met.

But right now your deaf/blind child is still a baby—his whole life lies before you. You will be surprised how soon the disabilities fade into the background. I *know* my deaf/blind daughter is handicapped, very handicapped, by her deaf/blindness (although as much due to lack of early help available to me as from her disability), but I do not *think* of her as handicapped, I think of her as 'Bunty', as she is, and love her for being herself. When I taught multiply handicapped preschoolers, I helped them most when I forgot about their disabilities and they became 'children', all with

their own lovable characters. First and foremost, your deaf/blind baby is a person and his deaf/blindness is part of him and in no way lessens the person he has the potential to be. He is a member of your family no less than any other child in it. He may bring some special problems, but he will also bring special joy. Love him and help him to learn to be as independent as possible and he could ask for no better parents. Now is the moment when the most important question to be asked is 'How do I begin?', and I hope you will find some of the answers in the following chapters. Turn to the programme and get started. Then, when you have time, read through the explanations in the intervening chapters as these will help you understand the reasons for what you are doing and enable you to see more clearly the path ahead which you and your child will travel along 'hand-on-hand'.

Remember, the left-hand column shows the activity to which the text refers or the experiences which the activity provides for your child. The right-hand column shows you how to go about the activity and gives you an explanation as to why the experiences provided for your child are important.

7

2 The problems and needs of the deaf/blind child

All the knowledge any one of us possesses has been received through our five senses. It is stored in our memory, first as images and later as words because this allows for more efficient storing. Touching, smelling and tasting are called 'near senses' because the information they convey is the result of actual contact with the body. By far the greatest information is received through our vision and hearing because, in addition to information close by, these two senses can tell us about things that are outside and at a distance from us. For instance, we can *see* things in the environment without the need to touch them, be near them or even be involved with them—they can be soundless and odourless yet we see them (e.g. the climber on the mountain). We can *see* what other people do and, by their behaviour, determine what we can and should do. We can *hear* things without the source being visible (the radio in the next room); we can *hear* the spoken thoughts of others and learn how they feel—and what we *hear* influences the way we think and the way we behave. It is through *hearing* that we learn to recognise the sounds of speech and to express our own thoughts and to communicate with others through this medium. To respond to the information we receive we must move—speech is movement, walking, writing, everything we do is the result of moving some part of our body. Although we discover for ourselves what to do with our body in order to perform an action, we also receive information about how to move by *seeing* others perform or by *hearing* what we are told to do.

Movement

No other sensory channel can take in so much information all at once as can vision—you cannot always feel the whole of an object at one and the same time, but you can see it all at once. Some visual information cannot be received by the other senses: things that are too large, like clouds, or too dangerous, like fire. Hearing too has unique qualities for it is the only sense that can literally bend round corners and attend to several inputs at the same time, e.g. we can be listening to someone talking to us while being aware that the radio is on in the next room and the baby is crying upstairs.

Vision and hearing have special functions

It is the information from our senses together with our ability to move that allow us to build up a stable picture of our world within which we can function and participate confidently.

8

The joy of movement.

Information   With impairment in both vision and hearing, the deaf/blind child's most valuable sources of information are restricted. It is rare to find a total loss in both channels, so he will get some information but it is likely to be incomplete or distorted. He therefore does not acquire a constant picture of the world he lives in nor models on which to base the way he behaves. He is unlikely to know what is around him, what is going on around him or even that he is part of it—his world may be one of ever-changing chaos unless we intervene and provide the necessary information in a form which makes sense to him. If we do not intervene, his world is likely to remain the world of his own body—outside himself nothing exists, there is no reason to explore or communicate. He creates his own stability by doing the same thing all the time—ritualistic activities with light stimulation or the same toy played with the same way day after day. He does not form real images of the world—things do have meaning for him but only as they appeal to his body and fit into his pleasure world. Such a child lacks distinction between himself and other things around him, he is not motivated to explore or to make relationships. It cannot be easy for the deaf/blind child to come to terms with living in a world where other people depend on their sight and hearing to respond to the demands made upon them. When he does fall back on his own resources, we may have to entice him by joining in his world, showing him we can also do what he does and that he can do the things we do. If we can provide him with the right kind of information for his stage of development and make his world interesting and meaningful, this kind of inward turning does not occur.

For us there is certainty in the knowledge that dinner will follow breakfast, day will follow night, that seven days after one awful Monday washing day there will be another awful Monday washing day, that if we 'go for a walk' we intend to return home, that if we wave bye-bye to Daddy when he goes to work, we can expect him to return in the evening, etc. The deaf/blind child does not have this kind of certainty unless we deliberately provide routine situations with clues he can recognise. Only this way can his life stop being a series of unexpected happenings and have a pattern which can be relied upon to recur. When he has this kind of reassurance we can introduce small changes and he will learn to accept these.

The deaf/blind child lacks the certainty that allows him to feel secure

He needs to have someone beside him, sharing their eyes and ears with him, interpreting the environment for him in a form that he can understand. This has to go on until he can feel secure in knowing what to expect to happen and its relationship to him; in knowing how to behave and what is expected of him. Our role as parents, indeed of all who along the way will help a deaf/blind person, is that of an *interpreter*—the 'in' word for this is 'intervener'. This definition is good, I believe, because it draws our attention to the fact that we do not have to think *what* kind of information we should provide for the child; he needs to know about everything that is going on around him, every object that is within his reach, what he can do with it and what effect this has. Not special information, just that which any other child would have; it lies all around him every minute of his waking day.

He needs interveners

We must remember, however, that information by itself is of little use, it is what you can do with knowledge that is important. You could 'tell' a deaf/blind child about a hole in a fence, a piece of wood, a hammer and a nail, but unless you showed him that the hole could be mended by covering it with a piece of wood which was held in place by hammering a nail through it, the information would have little meaning. So information must be given step by step, each piece being related, so that the child is able to develop understanding of the whole and make use of what he has learned.

Information must be integrated

Although at all times we encourage the child to use his residual vision and hearing and provide every possible opportunity for this, the deaf/blind child's main source of information is usually through touch. It is not as efficient a way of receiving or storing information as is sight and hearing, so, certainly in the early days, learning will be slower. What you can 'see' can be taken in at a glance, it can be described in a few words—recognising and remembering features by touch require a lot of effort and much time.

To pass on information tactually we use a simple method, and it is imperative that you do use it. It was first used in Holland, where it is called 'co-active movement'; in the United States it is called 'hand-over-hand', and in Canada 'hands-on', which is the term we use. All it means is that we pass on information to the deaf/blind child by using our hands on his. Whether it is information about an object, showing him how to do something or communicating with him to tell him something, it is done this way. This method is well documented in the book by McInnes and Treffrey (see book list, p. 142).

Hands-on those of the deaf/blind child

The position for 'hands-on' work is with the child's back to you, this way not only do your hands guide his, but in addition he gets clues as to how to position the rest of his body for the activity through the positioning of your body. This way you also:

convey more information than when working from the front,

direct the child in the activity at the natural angle which is more comfortable for him (if you make it awkward, he is less likely to co-operate),

The value of 'hands-on' method

have greater control over him—you can position your body so that it cuts out things which might distract his attention,

can use your body to guide his head to where you want him to *look*,

are in the best possible position to speak directly into the child's ear or within a suitable distance from his hearing aid.

For a very young baby you must work first with him on your

lap, later with him between your legs while you sit on the floor, or behind him as he sits in his high chair, or at a small table. Gradually you can move to a position at his side, but still with the ability to guide both his hands from behind should he need prompting.

Objects

With your hands on his, the child needs you to help him identify those features which will assist him in recognising and remembering an object, for instance the hollowness which is common to all things from which we can drink; the shape (low, long with a bump at one end) which identifies all beds and makes them different from things you can sit on (chairs, stools, settee—what is common to these?); the roundness that is common to balls, plates, saucers, wheels etc., and the differences which determine how each of these round things is used (made of different materials).

Actions

When concerned with actions, he needs you to show him how to do things with your hands on his. Self-care activities (such as feeding, dressing, undressing, washing etc.) and fine motor activities (such as banging, squeezing, pushing, threading, wind-up toys, jigsaws and so on) must all be demonstrated in this way. And you continue this until such time as, through your hands, you feel the child developing an anticipation of what has to be done next—at that stage you can lessen the help until he can take over the activity and do it by himself. Generally we try to encourage him to do the last part of an activity by himself, e.g. pull off the sock you have together pulled down and over the heel. Then, when he can do this, you encourage him to do the last two parts, and so on, until he has learned to do the whole independently—this is called 'back-chaining'.

Once an activity is thoroughly understood and can be completed by the child, a problem-solving situation can be introduced by slightly altering the task to make him think. He must, of course, have had experience of all the components and understand their relationship to each other. He needs to have a lot of successful experiences so that his confidence grows—some children lack natural curiosity and challenge in new experiences and many resent the new within the familiar, and it is up to us to recognise their difficulties and help them over them.

Allow him to do for himself when ready

It is very important that we never do for a deaf/blind child what he can do for himself (even as a time saver for our sake). However, we must be certain that we have given him sufficient know-how and practice for him to be able to perform the skill successfully. It is also very important that we do not just show a child how to do something and then forget to draw his attention to the effect of what he has done. He must understand what has been achieved by what he has done whether this is good, bad or an absolute disaster!

I think it helps in working 'hands-on' if you regard the activity you are sharing with your child as a sequence of movements which together make a pattern. The Swiss psychologist Piaget,

Patterns of movement

from his studies of young children, surmised that initially babies move their hands randomly and follow these visually. Eventually, as they learn to control the movements of their hands, they are able to repeat these patterns, which they both enjoy and find useful. First (he says) these are single patterns, then the child uses a series of patterns as a whole action (e.g. reaching for a rattle) and practises these again and again. Next he uses an action pattern to achieve an end (gets the rattle so he can play with it), then uses different actions to see their effect and find new ways of using them (bangs the rattle as well as shaking it). Finally the child anticipates the result of his actions before he does them, and uses them 'automatically' in new situations. A child who is unable to see and hear the result of his actions will not be motivated to repeat them.

This sequence of development, from making a simple single pattern to the ability to use several together in complex patterns to meet new situations, must be achieved by the deaf/blind child without vision. It is we who, with our hand on his, will be teaching him the sequences which made up the pattern of movement he needs to know. For instance, feeding himself involves a sequence of 11 movements each time he takes a mouthful—he has to:

locate the dish
find the spoon
grasp the spoon
put the spoon in the dish
scoop the food on to the spoon
bring the spoon up to his mouth
open his mouth
put the spoon in his mouth
take the food off the spoon
take the spoon out of his mouth
bring the spoon down to the dish . . .

and begin the sequence all over again. It is by doing the same set of actions again and again that they become established in the brain and can be called into use automatically. If *we* recognise the pattern of movements in an activity, we are more likely to keep to the same pattern each time we demonstrate it with the child. We are also more likely to be aware of the child being ready to take over part for himself, to begin back-chaining and encourage him towards independence. When he has learned to do an activity for himself, he will add to it his own characteristics or take short cuts, just as we all do.

When we are concerned with communication, the hands-on technique is most relevant, for the method of communication usually needed by the deaf/blind child is signing. It is now generally recognised that if you wait for a deaf/blind child to learn

13

Communication

to use speech for communication, he may end up very frustrated and with no means of communication at all. It is better from the first to give him an alternative means, but at the same time always giving him the opportunity to hear (and *see* it if this is possible) speech alongside the signing, so that if the potential is there, he will transfer to the use of the spoken language when he is ready and able.

In fact, hand movements are a lot easier to imitate than the very complex movements of the tongue, mouth, breath and larynx, all of which have to be co-ordinated to produce speech sounds. The child receives our messages by us manipulating his hands to form
Signs
the signs. As time goes on, the child will realise that we can receive his message by 'seeing' his signs, but at first we should encourage him to manipulate our hands when he wants to communicate with us. Just as he would need to hear words many many times before he could speak them, so our deaf/blind child will need to be shown how to make signs many many times in their correct context, before he will be able to make them and use them meaningfully.

Signs are also patterns of movements and should be thought of as having four parts which have to be made clear to the child if he is to be able to imitate them without the aid of vision—these are:

the shape the hand(s) make
the place of the body or space where the sign is made
the movement or flow of movement or actions of the hand(s)
the final hand shape in the act of completing the sign.

Remember that in all these aspects of tactile work, the child is 'seeing' through your manipulations—they must be clear, repeated many times, and must refer to something that is meaningful to the child.

Receiving information tactually requires that a child moves his hands, but the extent of his knowledge about the world would be very limited if he did not learn to move other parts of his body and become a moving person. Once a seeing baby sits and can grasp things, his vision of the world is so inviting that he needs no other
The deaf/blind have no reason to become mobile and explore
incentive to crawl, kneel, pull himself up and walk to explore it all. How different for the deaf/blind child: for him there is no reason to change from his nice safe position lying on his back. His movements do not become flexible because he does not turn his head to look at things or because of what he hears. When he does sit, there is nothing to encourage him to seek beyond the circle of his arms.

He needs us to show him what movements he can make with the various parts of his body and what can be achieved by making these movements, from discovery and problem solving to communication; what freedom he has once he can move on his own. Here too, we—the interveners—must manipulate the child through the movements until he can do them by himself and use them automatically to achieve his desires. At first we must not ask him to do these on his own—space is frightening when you do not know what is there. You must go with him, share the movement so that he feels safe, roll with him, crawl with him, jump with him, until he knows what to do and masters the skill—and does it because being physically active is both pleasant and useful. When he begins to move out into space, we must go with him at first—as we do this he will learn that things stay in their place and it is he who moves. As Dr Jan van Dijk (the Dutch specialist on deaf/blind children) says so eloquently: 'The child learns to make adjustments in space (to go round obstacles or to avoid them), he gets a sense of distance and this all helps to create an awareness of self. He can say "*I* go, *I* do", a spoon becomes not just a knocking thing, but the thing *I* eat with; he and things assume an identity and the world begins to have shape and form as well as people.' The chaos is getting sorted out.

The deaf/blind child has the same need for discipline as any other child in the family: if you make too many allowances for his disability, he will expect this from others and outside the home limits are much more finely drawn. Involvement with 'people' is essential for all of us; communication is the key to socialising and companionship, together with friendliness and acceptable behaviour, getting on with people—all areas of difficulty for the deaf/blind child and for those of us who are helping him to learn about them.

Discipline

As with any child, there will always be moments when the deaf/blind child is doing something that cannot be allowed to continue. Limits have to be set, and once you have said '**no**' you must not change your mind, but you must try to convey to the child your reason for your demand.

It is not necessary to discipline the very young child, but once he is crawling and walking occasions do arise, and it is then the best time for the child to learn that you mean what you say. When he does do something that he should not, make sure before you reproach him that he really has understood what he has done: have you taught him that that thing was wrong and, if you have, did he understand? Do not react too strongly or he may be frightened because he has missed all those clues that would have warned him—your cross face, the change in your tone of voice, your whole attitude as you went towards him. You can convey a lot of what you feel through your hands and the way you just hold him to express your disapproval, and by the vibrations of your cross voice—and these are good ways of indicating to him that he has misbehaved. Show him what it is you disapprove of, the consequences of his action and, if possible, let him help you put it to right again.

Deaf/blind children have temper tantrums the same as other children; here again, we need to examine the situation in which the child becomes upset because it might not in fact be a temper tantrum. It is possible to identify five occasions when a deaf/blind child might wrongly be thought to be having a tantrum.

> *Justified anger*: something had happened to him without warning—he needs to be given the information that allows him to accept the change.
> *Spoilt child*: the child who has always got what he wanted by making a fuss and will go on doing this as long as it gets him what he wants.
> *Unhappy child*: has a need for physical comfort but cannot tell you this.
> *Insecure child*: uses this negative way of getting attention—needs loving.
> *Protesting child*: is communicating and no one is taking any notice.

A real tantrum occurs when there is just too much frustration or anxiety for the child to bear and he blows an emotional fuse—once it has started it is difficult to stop, and often the child is terrified by the way he feels. He needs to be reassured: keep calm and, if he is small, you can hold him closely until he can regain control of himself. When a real tantrum is over, he may need to sleep or have a warm drink as he will be exhausted. Try to do something you know he likes so that he knows you understand.

Praise for good behaviour is better than taking abnormal notice of bad behaviour—a sweet for good behaviour, not for stopping the wrongdoing. If a sweet or a reward of some kind is given, this practice must be consistent and immediate and gradually dropped before it becomes a habit—the good behaviour has to

Inappropriate behaviour
become the habit. As regards inappropriate behaviour as opposed to 'naughty' behaviour, this is where learning to observe your child is important. Too often we credit these children's behaviour to something *we* think is the reason, forgetting that what *we think* is the result of *our* experience, experiences which are likely to be very different from those our deaf/blind child will have had. We must watch and see what leads to the behaviour, how often does it occur, what is it he actually does and in what circumstances—the answers to questions like these will enable us to correct the behaviour by removing the cause or offering an alternative which is acceptable to the child.

We should always remember that as the child learns and progresses and begins to be in control of his world, his behaviour will change at a faster rate than his understanding so that, lacking language to reason with, he does not control his behaviour easily and becomes more difficult to handle for a while. This is when we need to be very patient and understanding.

Rewards do not, of course, only result when we do something right as opposed to something wrong. Pleasure is a reward, and if we do something that gives us pleasure, we are more likely to want to do it again and to learn from doing it. When we grow up we accept that it is often necessary to do things we do not like because of the reward it brings us, e.g. a boring job that is well paid. The reward for a seeing, hearing child may be in the manipulation of the material he plays with, or seeing the result of his work or the pleasure in our faces coupled with our verbal praise of his skill, and so on. For the deaf/blind child, so many of these rewards do not exist unless we draw his attention to them, provide a form of reward such as a big hug, or make sure that the task or the way we present the task has a built-in reward that is meaningful to him. We need to watch for those activities that specially please him and use these as a reward. For new tasks, he needs to be rewarded for a good try, then when it is completed; but as soon as it is easily done, reward every so often—by then you would be introducing the next stage and the reward would be transferred to this and faded out completely for the original task. A deaf/blind child will use his residual vision and hearing if doing this results in reward, and he will want to do things with us and for us if our pleasure in his achievements is rewarding to him—a hug, a romp or a pat on the head can be as effective as a Smartie for many of these children.

Reward

For every young child, play is learning and learning is play—although neither he nor we tend to think of it that way. It comes naturally to a child because he is curious, he wants to practise his skills and try them out in new ways, and he is interested in and wants to imitate what he sees others doing. If his play is not purposeful, there is something wrong with him. He plays wherever he is and stops only when involved in some routine event—even then it is sometimes very hard to prise him away from his play, so strongly does it absorb him. He often comes to us for help and approval, but on the whole, in the early stages, likes to play by himself or alongside his brothers and sisters, only later learning to share his activities with his contemporaries. Play is a very important part of every child's education, no less for those who are deaf/blind, but it is pretty obvious from the difficulties we have already highlighted that he is unlikely to play purposefully unless we teach him how—and we can only do that by playing with him.

Play

Everything you do with your child has to be enjoyed by you both, but as you will have realised, to help the deaf/blind child to the greatest extent, nothing can be done haphazardly. Play periods with the very young child are mostly physical activities, but once he is sitting up and is awake for considerable periods, he needs to handle objects which have those qualities by which he will later recognise things (e.g. round things, things with different textures as well as rattles, noisemakers and so on), but he will need you to guide him. Later, he will need toys which he can activate or do something with so that they change (hammer and pegs). What he learns will be different from what the seeing, hearing child learns—the wind-up car for him cannot represent a

17

model of his Daddy's car, it is a thing 'which when I wind it up, moves', for no way can he relate the model to the real thing unless he has a great deal of sight. So play things need to be carefully thought about. Short periods of play together which occur at regular intervals each day are preferable to begin with, and play should be with the same objects until the child has become familiar with them—they can then be the things he plays with by himself, for free play and opportunity to do what he wants are also necessary.

This chapter has described some of the basic ways of learning which are denied to the deaf/blind child and some of the things which we need to think about if we are to provide alternatives that are meaningful to him.

As you work through the programme, you will find these alternatives in practical terms and you will be surprised how soon it becomes habit to play with your child with a purpose in mind, as much because he is responding with understanding as because of your growing confidence. In the next chapter we will look at some sources of information which are close at hand.

3   *Sources of information for interveners*

Confronted with the task of bringing up a deaf/blind child, it is only natural that we seek information that will help us. Books, courses, conferences, teachers, other parents have a great deal to offer us, yet there are three valuable sources which we should not ignore and which are readily available. These are:

the child himself
the experiences of seeing/hearing children
your own experiences.

The child himself

How can the child himself guide us in what we should be doing with him? Well, if we are to provide him with information, we must also know he is receiving it or we are wasting our time. We must know that the child is responding to us, and we can only do this if we observe him very carefully. Often his response is brief, sometimes not at all what we expect, and even a negative response at least tells us what he does not like. Working 'hands-on' with your young deaf/blind child you do become very aware of changes in his behaviour which indicate he is responding to you.

Observation for response and readiness

It may be no more than a stilling of his body to show that he is listening, or a slight body movement to show you he wants to go on with the activity you are sharing, or pressure of a finger to show you he is ready to take on board a bit of an activity. This is his only way of communicating with you to begin with, and if you do not observe him carefully and miss this, he is likely to stop trying because he thinks you are not responding to him. His responses are saying 'I get the message. What comes next?' Knowing what comes next is of little use unless you know, by observing his behaviour, the child is ready for it.

Relationships

Communicating is a reciprocal action. It occurs between two people between whom there is a relationship within which each is aware of the other's identity. Before any child can know he is a person, he needs to recognise another person as separate from himself, and generally this is mother. Sight and hearing play a major part in the development of this relationship, so the deaf/blind child is at a tremendous disadvantage. With him it is not a simple 'I love you' relationship, it is a 'this is *me*' relationship which draws attention to all those things about you which make you '*you*'. When you become familiar to him in all

19

these aspects and by your activities with him, he gradually learns to trust you and enjoy being with you and wants to please you—and this is a stage he must reach before he is ready to learn from the things you do together. You represent a part of that stability that he so greatly needs. You may have to work at this relationship making—it is not easy to keep smiling at a baby who does not smile back because he cannot see your smile—and pour out your love at a rate of knots. It will penetrate and, because you are watching for it, you *will* find that he is responding; when you show him by your response that you know this, you are well away and communication has begun. It is only by observing his seeing behaviour that you will learn if, what, where and when he is using his vision, and you must know this if you are to encourage visual skills. It is only by observing his response to sound that you will know if he is listening and what he listens to, and it is only by listening to the sounds he makes that you will know which sounds he recognises. It is only by being aware of the movements his hands make beneath yours that you will know he is learning what to do.

Observing your child tells you a great deal about him. If we do not watch out for this information, we may miss his readiness to advance and fail to provide the necessary opportunity and experience. He is a mine of information—dig deep. The programme in this book includes some ideas of what to look for as the child progresses from stage to stage.

The second most valuable guide to what to do with a deaf/blind child is not so much the developmental stages through which all children pass (although you should know these), but those experiences which enable a child to progress from stage to stage. The deaf/blind child needs to have these same experiences and we have to provide them in such a way that he too learns the skills. In

Experiences of normal children

play and imitation, children have lots of opportunity for practising, refining and consolidating what they have learned; the deaf/blind child must have these opportunities too. From use of a skill in a single context, children seek to use it in broader and ever more complex situations—we must provide these situations for the deaf/blind child.

I once watched a 4-year-old deaf/blind girl and her 2-year-old brother. She ran aimlessly about the room, climbing up to windows and on to furniture. He sat at a small table on which there were some cups and saucers and spoons ready for later on. First he put all the spoons into one cup, then into the next, then he put one spoon in each cup, the saucers in a pile, the cups together, then one cup on each saucer together with a spoon. He was completely absorbed in his play, within which the skills of number, position, sorting, estimating, having fun and many others were all being experienced. These are the kinds of self-initiated practice situations from which children learn so much, but which are not part of the deaf/blind child's experience

20

unless we deliberately provide them for him. You do not need a lot of expensive equipment: suitable things are all around you and familiarising the deaf/blind child with these increases his awareness of everyday things. Show him 'hands-on' what he can do with things, what you do with them, where they are kept, what they are used for, give him time to play with things in a variety of ways so that you are extending his experiences and preparing him for more complex uses of basic skills. From the little boy's play with the tea things would come an awareness of when they are used, and what for, where they are kept, how cared for, where bought, their cost, and so on ad infinitum. From the simple activity of learning to put things in a box grows the skill of, say, putting away your shoes in the cupboard, and from knowing where your shoes are kept comes the ability to fetch them yourself if you know you are going out or as a sign that you want Mummy to take you out. So much that has to be learned comes from the experiences of everyday living—it may be easier to let the deaf/blind child sit safely in the middle of the room with his favourite toy, but if you do, you take away his chance of learning about the world he lives in and how to act independently in it.

Everyday activities and objects

If you have other children in your family, observe the way they play and what they do, and try to provide the same experiences for your deaf/blind child, or at least similar. If you have no other children within the family, observe children in a preschool or playgroup. It will be time well spent, and the knowledge you gain, when added to what you know about your deaf/blind child, will provide a good guide to the kind of things you need to do with him.

Family or playgroup

In passing on information 'hands-on' you are of necessity passing on your *own* experiences. These may tend to be visual rather than tactile—and that which is a salient feature visually may not be so tactually. For instance, how do you convey to a deaf/blind child the function of a mirror? We might recognise a box by the fact that it is square and therefore has corners, but to put a deaf/blind child's hands on each corner would not convey sufficient information—he needs to put his hands around it to judge its size, move from corner to corner, preferably with some reference mark at the first corner to let him know when he is back at the beginning. Even that would not give him sufficient information unless he had had lots of experience of squareness before.

Your own experiences

If we are to provide information tactually, we must make *ourselves* tactually aware—that is, *feel* for ourselves objects and actions so that we know exactly what it is necessary to alert the child to in order for the information to be useful. In this way our own experiences help us to know what to pass on to our child.

It is important to be aware of just how much 'touch' means to all of us—we are inclined to think of it as a minor source of information. Yet by touching and moving we learn about such

21

Importance of touching and being touched

Body contact

Temperature

Pressure

Emotions

Vibration

things as texture, shape, weight and, by being touched, the way people react and feel about us, to name but a few. Most of us never stop to think much about the function of our skin, although it is the largest of our sensory organs for it covers all of us (it is the only one we could not do without!), and under each piece the size of a 5p piece there are at least 50 nerve ends carrying messages to our brain. Think how much it appears in the phrases we use in our daily conversations—people rubbing us up the wrong way, get in touch, a pat on the back, losing our grip, clutching at straws, and so on. Body contact is the new baby's first form of communication and it is very important to his socialising and relationship experiences. It is his first contact with the outside world, and from this grows his readiness to accept new experiences. Temperature we are aware of through our skin—being too hot or too cold is unpleasant, harmful sometimes—observing what suits the deaf/blind child best and trying to meet his needs in this respect may make all the difference to his comfort and therefore his receptiveness. Pressure is another way of conveying information—it can be an efficient way of remembering certain things, particularly if you are on the receiving end, e.g. a slap conveys a very different message from a caress. Pressure may be a means by which a deaf/blind child learns to identify people—in handling him we give him information, from our body to his, in terms of intensity, rhythm, duration and firmness. Tension is another source of information which we can convey through our body—anxiety, anger, frustration—and if we do feel this way, we should ask someone else to take over the deaf/blind baby until we have controlled our feelings and can approach him calmly again.

Vibrations which can be felt through our body inform us of people approaching by their footsteps (and these are different for each of us), when vehicles are approaching, the rhythms of loud music, machines and speech sounds, and so on.

Every minute of the day that a seeing/hearing child is not eating, sleeping, involved in daily routines or a teaching situation, he is occupied in active exploration of his environment—it should be equally so for the deaf/blind child. Long ago, J. J. Rousseau wrote: 'Touch is always busy, during waking hours it is spread over the whole of the body like a sentinel, ever on watch'. Think of it like this when you are with your deaf/blind child—it is his lifeline. Become aware of how much of your own behaviour is related to touch so that you can pass this on to your child. Train yourself to notice salient features of things by touch alone (with your eyes closed); to recognise people other than by seeing them; to be aware of what is happening without depending on being able to see and hear. In this way you will realise that your own experiences are indeed a real source of help in knowing what a deaf/blind child needs to know. Try not to *see* things, but see how they *feel*.

4 Development and functions of vision and hearing

Because these are areas in which our child has an impairment, we need to be well informed about the function, development and skills involved and to understand the effect of the impairment.

Let us look first at vision. Seeing is so natural to us that we do not always appreciate how rich a source of information it is. Like touch, it figures frequently in our language: we did not see eye to eye, seeing is believing, the apple of his eye, he caught my eye; descriptive phrases, such as a black look, wild eyes, dewy eyed; eyes register emotion—surprise, hostility, guilt, horror, bewilderment, and so on. These examples highlight some of the things a deaf/blind child is likely to miss.

We look at what we want to see

None of us gathers visual information randomly, we seek for that which we want to see in order to satisfy and realise our own objective: if we are looking along the street to see if Johnny is coming home from school, we do not notice how many cars are parked along the way or other irrelevances, our vision is seeking for the little figure with the satchel on his back. Deaf/blind children need to be taught to look at what is relevant to their experience.

Deaf/blind make mental 'maps'

Sighted children learn easily to discriminate objects because these are usually within a framework they can see in detail, can be expected to be there or may be there permanently. A deaf/blind child has to explore the parts to create the idea of a whole, and only by travelling between and around and with objects over and over again can he gain a kind of mental image to supplement any visual image he may have. Before language can develop, a child has to have many mental images of things in his world.

Visual development sequence

From the normal child's sequence of growing visual efficiency, we know that his first visual reaction is to a light source. The child then learns to fixate, that is to look at an object of interest without attending to other things in the surroundings—he seems to be staring steadily at things for quite a time. Next he learns to follow a person or thing moving at one side or the other, soon from side to side across the midline. He begins to watch his own fingers and if he is held in the sitting position, can follow an object moving up and down. Soon he is able to move quickly and exactly from one fixation to another, regardless of whether he is still or moving, to learn to move his eyes to see without moving his head. This ability

23

to track is vital because, of course, none of us sees by looking directly at an object, although we may think we do—we actually take in all its aspects by rapid tracking in order to 'see' the thing as a whole. The child learns to focus—that is, to use both eyes together and to adapt his vision to take account of distance. Gradually he learns to recognise people, objects, places, colours, shapes. By doing visual training activities and by creating situations within normal routines to encourage him to look at and look for things, we can help the child with poor, but useful, vision go through these stages.

Eyes need using

Eyes benefit by being used, otherwise the pathways to the brain will atrophy and become useless. The urge to see is very strong in all of us. When we do not help the deaf/blind child to find meaning in what he sees, his burning need for a visual input often leads to stereotype light gazing habits which become obsessive and get in the way of learning.

There are many different conditions leading to impairment of vision, and these may each have a different effect on the way a child is able to see. Unless a child is obviously totally blind, the fact that initially he does not seem to respond to a visual input does not necessarily mean he cannot see. Even an awareness of the difference between light and dark can become of use to a child in itself, but it is always a sign that there is some vision there. Only by encouraging its use will we learn how much and how useful—and this can take some considerable time.

The smallest bit of vision can be useful

In order to be able to train the deaf/blind child to develop the early visual skills, we need to observe his behaviour very closely indeed. The ophthalmologist will be able to tell us whether the child lacks peripheral vision and therefore cannot see without turning his head; lacks central vision and therefore sees best from the corners and is not able to look directly at something to see it; or lacks vision in any one area of his eyes, e.g. if in the lower field, he will not see things put directly in front of him, they need to be in front but further away.

Necessary information

This information, together with our own observations, will tell us the best position in which to hold objects we want the child to look at or pick up, and we must know this before we can begin any activity using or training vision. A child's behaviour gives us many clues: if he responds to a torch light, reaches without fumbling, holds things close to his eyes, sees things in the distance but bumps into things in the way. Unlike speech, from which we can deduce information about a hearing loss by comparing with the normal, we cannot know exactly what a child sees (if he is unable to communicate with us) except by observing how he uses his sight, and he may not use it until we have trained him to do this. We must always remember that it is the reaction of the muscles in our eyes that triggers off those in our body required to bring the eye into the position where we can see best. The deaf/blind child may lack this automatic positioning, so we must encourage him by showing him how to position himself to look—if he can learn to do this, it will help to use his vision more efficiently. Also, if he has central vision yet looks away from what he is doing, it may mean he is operating tactually because he finds this preferable and maybe easier—concentrating visually is known to be very tiring.

Wearing visual aids

Some children these days have soft lenses from a very early age instead of glasses, and it is to be hoped that this will become standard practice where possible as it avoids problems that often arise from wearing glasses. However, glasses are necessary still for some children. If a child has had cataracts and the lens removed, he will see nothing clearly without a contact lens or glasses. When the lenses have not been removed, the child may, for close work, see better without glasses: the more a child looks at close range, the more he is likely to see. If he does not do this naturally, he must be shown how to bring things close enough. When a child first has glasses or the prescription is changed, or he has undergone an eye operation, things with which he has become familiar may initially appear distorted. He may not want to wear his glasses and may take them off. We should not force him to put them back, but wait for an opportunity to do something he enjoys sharing which is visually stimulating and meaningful and put them back on then. Visual tasks need to be within the visual competence of the child and we cannot engineer this unless we know the condition of the eyes and make careful observations of his seeing behaviour.

Visual perception

Just putting glasses on a child will not make him see. Seeing and interpreting what you see are separate functions in the brain. A child could *see* a picture of a spoon, but still not understand that what he sees (perceives) is the same object as that with which he feeds himself. It is by bringing together the information he gets about a spoon from seeing it, feeling it, using and naming it, that the spoon becomes *spoon*, whether two or three dimensional, whatever its size or shape, whatever it is made of or used for and from whichever way it is viewed. We must draw the deaf/blind child's attention to all these aspects if he is to *perceive* what he sees.

Object permanence

Vision plays an important part in many of the early learning stages, and we should know about the effect an impairment has on these. The first stage is *object permanence*—that is, knowing that things are there whether they are present or not. The baby drops his rattle, he watches it roll until it is out of sight under a chair, he watches Mummy retrieve it from under the chair and give it back to him; or she hides it under a cushion and he finds it; or when he watches her go out of sight through the doorway, he watches for her to come back through the doorway. This is all part and parcel of a child's security, knowing that things exist permanently, and that he is separate from them, that they can be expected to be in their place, being able to imagine them when

25

they cannot be seen. The child with a visual impairment who does not see where an object has gone will not know where to find it again, or even know that he could. If he is also deaf, you cannot tell him what is happening either. When he throws a toy it has gone—for ever. He does not know when we hand it back to him that it is the same one that he threw away. Unless we encourage him to search and show him where it has rolled to and that it is still present, he does not learn to search for things (and this is an essential ingredient of incentive to explore and become mobile), nor does he learn to understand his own location and direction. Without a good grasp of object permanence, a child will not develop good memory skills. Until a child has awareness that an object continues to exist, he cannot be expected to localise sound, nor point to it (which is a recognised stage in communication).

Cause and effect

Secondly, it is by *seeing* that a child realises his hands can be used to get things and to do things, to manipulate other tools and so achieve what he desires. It is what he *sees* that encourage a child to reach out and grasp the rattle he wants. It is when he sees the relationship between a piece of string and the toy to which it is attached that he will understand its role in getting him the toy. Here also is an area in which we must make sure *we* provide experiences through which a deaf/blind child will learn these concepts without the use of vision. For instance, it is no good showing him how to pull a toy along unless he is fully aware of each part of the object by tactual exploration, so that he is aware that his actions on the string are what make the toy move along. If he is not aware of these things, pulling the toy will hold no interest and he will not be motivated to join in activities of this kind, which is unfortunate for within them lies the foundation of independence—'What *I* can do' and 'What *I* can do with things'.

Manipulation

If a child does not learn to manipulate various types of toys and objects and recognise their functions, differences and similarities, he cannot begin to sort them into categories and label them (associate a sign with them). If you cannot do this, you have to remember every single thing as a separate image, an impossibility for any normal memory, let alone one where the 'labels' are tactual ones. The deaf/blind child will use objects for self-stimulation if he is not shown how objects are used and encouraged to begin to store an array of images that will enable him to classify objects according to their functions.

Imitation

It is through *imitation* that children acquire many of the early learning skills and, of course, *seeing* what others are doing is a great motivator. Seeing Mummy smile sets off the baby's smiling response; seeing the message in her eyes, he responds with his eyes (a vital element in early relationship making). When the deaf/blind child's jaws are ready to chew, he does not have a model of the necessary actions and may be frightened of new textures or foods which he cannot see being enjoyed by others, so he remains on soft foods indefinitely. He cannot see how other people walk, so he may walk on his toes, with his feet turned out or with a downward posture of his head. The natural gestures which are part of our language and which we all use in expressing ourselves are not seen by deaf/blind children, so communication at its most simple level is denied them unless we show them. They do not have models for imaginative play—the little girl who baths her doll like Mummy baths the new baby—or any kind of play for that matter, unless we show them first how to act and then encourage them to copy.

When vision is integrated with tactile and kinaesthetic information (kinaesthetic=awareness of the movements we have made, are making, or plan to make), it provides us with what is called spatial ability. Because we have seen, felt, moved an object, we learn to recognise it from whatever angle we see it, e.g. we cannot see the back of a cup, but we know what it looks like all round. We can see objects in our way and automatically make the evading actions, we can see ourselves where we are in relation to the other things around us, and can imagine how we would need to move or move things in certain circumstances. Integration of all these skills is critical to teaching the child with a visual impairment how to learn and how to solve problems.

No less critical are those skills which the use of hearing allows us to develop, e.g. awareness of environmental sounds such as music/pleasure, vehicle approaching/danger, footsteps/someone approaching; and, more important almost, the ability to hear the spoken word from which develops the understanding of language, the ability to imitate and use it meaningfully. Having

Hearing

the double handicap from birth is a unique condition in itself, and methods suitable for children who are deaf can rarely be used satisfactorily initially. Deaf children depend on lipreading, facial and environmental clues if they are only partially so, and if the hearing loss is severe, need good vision to see manual signs. Fortunately, few deaf/blind children are totally deaf and if they are taught to use what they have, it can be very useful. It can be possible for some of these children to learn to understand the spoken word and respond to it, but still be unable to learn to use speech themselves—it is tempting to speak to such children and not to sign, but unless we do sign to them so that they learn the signs, they will have no way of communicating with us. As children become proficient in signing, they do develop speed, rhythm and phrasing to their signing similar to those in speech. Although we all use the same signs, each one of us has his own personal way of producing a sign, and the deaf/blind child will learn to recognise this in the same way as we recognise different people's voices.

Because hearing and speaking are so closely intertwined, we think of them as inseparable. They are, indeed, dependent on each other, but in the young baby they do develop in parallel for a while. Hearing is perhaps the most complex of all the areas, so it

27

may be helpful to understanding the development of auditory and speech skills if we look at the sequence in which each progresses to the stage where intellectual ability enables them to merge. What follows is a gross oversimplification, but it will perhaps enable you to see the sequences through which you must work.

Auditory skills (input—receptive)

Listening—awareness that there is sound (now there is sound, now there is no sound).

Recognition—I've heard that sound before (remembering).

Discrimination—I recognise this sound and that sound (they are not the same or they are the same).

Association—this sound belongs to this thing and that sound belongs to that thing, that is Mummy's voice, Daddy's car, the radio etc., that word means drink coming, bed means I go to sleep.

Speech skills (output—expressive)

Reflex sounds—these are the early cries the baby makes.

Babbling—experimental sounds which the baby makes and *hears* himself make and realises he is making them himself and practises them because he enjoys it.

Imitation—Mother copies her baby's sounds and encourages him to copy hers. She notices the sounds he makes which may contain some element of real words, so she gives him the correct word. The baby matches his sounds to hers and refines them.

First meaningful sounds—the baby discovers that when he makes certain sounds it gets him results, e.g. if he says 'ba' when his ball rolls out of reach, his Mum knows what he means and gets it for him.

It is important to realise that hearing the sounds he himself makes (like word sounds of others) is as necessary to the skills of speech as is hearing what others *say*. Also, that speech is a motor activity and until the child has developed the muscular ability to produce the complex movements of mouth, tongue, throat and larynx, he will not be able to speak as we do.

As I have said previously, although we must offer a deaf/blind child the opportunity to have those experiences which, if he has the ability, enable him to learn to use speech as a means of communication, alongside this we must also communicate with him by signing, to guard against having no means of communication at all if speech does not develop. Signing develops in parallel in the same way as hearing/speech;

Tactile input (receptive)

Movement pattern—awareness that his hands are being manipulated.

28

Recognition—remembers his hands have been moved in that way before.

Discrimination—recognises the differences between hand manipulations.

Association—this movement goes with drink; that movement means I am going to have something to eat.

Output movement (expressive)

'Reflex'—waves hands about randomly.

'Babble'—begins to control hands and fingers and move them together.

Imitation—copies bits of the various movement patterns he is aware of; will be helped to complete them and encouraged to do them by himself. Mother copies his natural gestures to begin with.

First meaningful signals/signs—finds that putting his hand to his mouth gets him a biscuit!

Whether we are encouraging communication by speech or by signing (and we should be doing both), it is when the last stage on the receptive side comes together with the last stage on the expressive side that communication at the highest level occurs. The child is using a word or sign to represent something that is not necessarily there but may be something he needs, has done or wants to do. Before this he will have communicated many many other times in other ways, and it is only by our noticing these and responding to them that he will keep trying and slowly work his way through the sequence I have outlined.

Where there is a visual disability as well, it is often difficult to test a child's hearing and get results that will give accurate information as to the extent of the loss and therefore the child's potential for speech. The fact that such a child does not appear to hear is not always an indication of a severe loss: a child can often hear but may not be listening, and absence of 'looking' behaviour makes it difficult to monitor listening. Quietness and immobility may not be disinterest—you need to become a 'hand-watcher' as movements of his hands may indicate that the child is paying attention to sound. Listening involves hearing, but also *attending* to what we hear. From a general mêlée a child has to become aware of those sounds which occur frequently (Mummy's voice, the door banging, the clock chiming etc.), and then discover where they come from and learn to associate and remember what they signify. Deafness makes listening hard—sounds may be fuzzy, only vowels may be heard, high or low sounds may not be heard. The deaf/blind child has difficulty in associating sound and source—he needs to know that the mouth is where the sound of the person speaking is coming from, that it changes shape and that by touching it there are vibratory clues *and* that all these sounds can become meaningful to him. Sounds by themselves are not meaningful; the deaf/blind child must touch, taste, smell, trace and manipulate the object at the same time as he hears its name or receives the sign for it many times if an association is to be made.

As a general rule, hearing aids are issued when it is felt that these will help the child. Today these may be radio aids with which the child can receive information from the speaker, who can be quite some distance away. This means the child is less isolated than when he has ordinary aids. With the body or post-aural aids now used for many years, although improving all the time, you need to be close to and at the level of the child's microphone when speaking to him—so while he is little *you* will have to spend a lot of time on your knees!

Remember, communication is not something you teach, it is learned by being used, it is the medium through which we teach. As such it is central to everything you do with your child. Communicating is generally the 'big thing' with deaf/blind children because, I suppose, the methods are less well known. But it is a 'big thing' for *all* children, without it they would learn little, for in addition to spoken language, it encompasses writing and reading that language. Since it develops in the seeing/hearing child with little apparent effort, we do not give it publicity apart from the natural joy at the first word. Once we understand how to communicate with a deaf/blind child and are able to show him how to make a response and initiate conversation for himself, I believe here too it should be regarded as natural and not overstressed. A language system is not just words, phrases and sentences, it is a process in which we guide the child in his exploration, help him make sense of and organise his environment. Before a child can label an object with a word or sign, he must have had repeated exposure to the object itself, matching and contrasting it with others so that he can pick out those features which identify it and possess an image with which to link it; a child, unless he understands what 'going to the toilet' actually requires him to do, could as easily take the word or sign 'toilet' to mean going to the bathroom or sitting on the toilet, neither of which would necessarily have the desired result. Without vision to clarify the link, we need to think carefully about the signs and the circumstances in which we use them so that we avoid confusion. If the child cannot learn to represent his images in a symbolic form (word or sign), his tools for thought remain very limited—thinking is only possible because we can condense the specific labels for things into sets for easy reference, e.g. a child who no longer counts his fingers has not stopped counting, he can do it in his head.

Another important aspect of language is its effect in controlling behaviour. The child who remembers his mother's words 'Don't touch that, it's hot' is able to control his desire to touch—a child without language will not have this inner control and may go on touching things that are dangerous many many times before he remembers all the circumstances that go to make up the unpleasant experience and so exert his own control.

Finally, let us not forget that learning is an everyday affair, and everyday living experiences are learning experiences. Hans Furth said: 'Knowledge is like a circle that never ends because once you know about an object, then you experience the object differently. Knowledge is a circle that does not go back into the same circle. It is self-expendable, with no absolute beginning or end. It is not just one answer nor is it tied to words. Language is not knowledge, it provides the occasion for receiving and sharing knowledge—all knowledge is that you do something.' The worst thing you can do to a deaf/blind child is to do nothing—if he does not see well enough to understand the relationships of what he sees and does not hear enough to be told about them, we *must* intervene or there will be only very limited learning.

The Programme

Stage 1

INTRODUCTION TO THE PROGRAMME AND TO STAGE 1

The premise upon which this programme is based is that we should be providing the experiences which enable the deaf/blind child to progress at his own pace through the sequence of normal milestones in order that he can develop to his true potential.

There have been developmental schedules and programmes specially related to the child who is deaf/blind, but they do not cover the very early years in great detail. In this programme, while stressing the development of the whole child, I have endeavoured to identify the various areas in which the deaf/blind child needs special help. As parents, we tend to look at the whole child and if we cannot see progress there, easily become depressed and less likely to continue our efforts. If we can recognise the different areas and see progress in one or two of these, we are encouraged to continue. It matters less that the progress is slow than that there is progress however small—given time and the appropriate stimulation, it will spread over into other areas.

All young children need time to assimilate information and to learn to use this, and it is recognised that there are certain times in the early years when children learn some things more easily than at any other time. Whereas we cannot expect a deaf/blind child to progress as quickly as a seeing/hearing child, we can most certainly begin preparing him as near as possible to that optimum time. This way, when he is ready to make the step forward, with our help he will have had those experiences which his deaf/blindness might otherwise have denied him. For example, no child will walk before he is physically ready, but the seeing/hearing child will have watched people walk and seen what walking enables them to do so that, when he is ready, he is motivated to imitate them. The deaf/blind child lacks this motivation unless we devise ways of giving him the experience through us and of showing him what being able to walk will achieve for him.

This programme cannot list every single thing you can or may wish to do, but it should have just enough ideas to set you thinking along the right lines and to enable you to take advantage of the wealth of opportunity there is for the deaf/blind child to learn from within his own family and home. Like any other child, the deaf/blind one will have his good and his bad days. No matter how carefully you plan your programme, the child is an individual and may sometimes want to do things differently or need to go back over an earlier stage; he must be allowed to have this freedom. As time goes on, you will get to know your child and know when you can relax and not lose ground. So if some days do not go exactly to plan, it does not mean that your programme is not working. Only if there is really persistent poor reaction should you question whether your child understands what is required of him and whether you should seek another way of putting over the same information which would suit him better. From long experience I can tell you that it is usually when you have decided to change an activity because it does not seem to be getting the desired results, that the child demonstrates the appropriate response!

This programme is *not* a tool for measuring progress; the stages represent only an arbitrary division. However, it is quite likely that some deaf/blind children will have completed it before the age of 3, and others may perhaps need a further year. Nowadays, many disabled children enter nursery school at about 3, and this is good both for the child and his mother. The child's horizons are widened to take in another environment which is geared to his needs as a preschooler, and the mother gets a break from the continuous care. The staff at such a nursery must be given the opportunity of studying the programme and should be shown by you, the parents, how to handle and communicate with your child. Continuity is absolutely essential, as is the need for you and the teachers to plan together the continuing programme. For the child to get the greatest benefit from both environments, you and the teachers must play roles that complement each other. The teacher introduces a new skill in the classroom, you provide opportunities for the child to practise this in everyday living situations in the home. Unless there is unity of purpose between all who come into contact with the child, he will not progress as well as he might.

But, as yet, your child is a long way off this stage, and we must begin at the beginning. The period we are now about to cover in **Stage 1** is probably the most difficult one for you his parents, because of the emotional adjustment you have to make, and it could be the easiest for your baby because it is a time when his main need is for love, food, warmth and a lot of sleep.

However, a lot of disabled babies do not have a good start. This is particularly so of those who are deaf/blind through maternal rubella (German measles in pregnancy), for they may still have to combat the effects of this infection for some time after birth (during which time, incidentally, they remain infectious and can

pass on the infection to others who come into contact with them).
Once the infection has died down, they pick up fairly quickly and
begin to make better progress. Other children with the dual
handicap from another or unknown cause may need hospital care
for a while immediately after birth, in which case it is not possible
for the close bonding with the mother to begin as early as
desirable. There may also be some who have additional problems
which make handling difficult.

For these reasons, Stage 1 does not make any great demands on
you or your baby and it can last until such time as he is fit enough
and you feel ready to begin the more intensive work. The stages of
the programme represent a gradual build up of skills, each one
preparing for the next. So it is important to begin at Stage 1,
remembering, if it has not been possible to start during the early
months, it cannot be assumed that your child will not have been
learning anything during that period. If he has been a sick child,
some of his experiences may not have been very pleasant, and he
is unlikely to have had the kind of consistent handling that helps
to make a child feel secure. Until his environment contains
pleasant experiences and he can recognise and learn to trust those
who care for him, he may resist efforts to stimulate him. The ideas
in Stage 1 will help this, whatever the age of your little one, so
begin there, take your time over it, and move on to Stage 2 only
when you feel you are both ready.

Right from the very first, we are going to offer the deaf/blind
baby the opportunity to hear speech and feel signs—which
method he will ultimately use for communication will depend on
the abilities he develops as he grows and progresses. With the
blind/deaf child, the signs are made with his hands and, where
there is vision enough, signs are made so that he can see them.
Many more people than just the deaf and deaf/blind use a sign
language these days, and their lives are greatly enhanced because
they have a means of contact with other human beings instead of
being isolated. Most of the signs we use are those of the British
Sign Language, but a vocabulary of signs appropriate for the
progressive development of signing called 'Maketon' will provide
you with illustrations of all those you are likely to need for the
time being. Where a particular sign is to be used, I have illustrated
this in the programme, but you will undoubtedly need more, so I
would recommend that you purchase a copy of Maketon from the
National Association Family Centre, whose address you will find
in the list of useful associations in Appendix 4 (p. 144). For
parents living in countries using different sign systems, I would
suggest that you make a small drawing of your own sign and
paste it over the square containing the British one.

During these early weeks, while your baby needs less of your
time, relax and rest as much as you can, for busy times lie ahead.
Read some of the books and familiarise yourself with Stage 1. The
more you help your baby in the early years, the more likely he will

be able to help himself later on. Talk to people about your baby—it is easy at this time to withdraw from your social life, yet it is really most important to keep and increase your friendships. Relatives and friends represent people who, if they have the need of the child explained to them, will be able to share in the task. For your sake and the child's, it will be necessary to seek the help of other people—interveners—for caring for and stimulating a disabled child requires us to give a lot of ourselves. It may be very satisfying to feel we can do everything and manage on our own; it is easy to get to the stage of believing no one else can handle the child as well as we can. This may be true, but once the child has made a good relationship with his mother and his father, he must learn to relate to other people, for he will need the help of many people along the pathway of life. While he is with other people, you must rest or get out and enjoy a social life so that you are refreshed and lively when it is your time to be with your child.

The main objectives of Stage 1 are: (1) to identify those things which occur automatically when a baby can see and hear but which, in the case of the deaf/blind child, we must consciously think about, (2) to get to know your baby and provide him with information that helps him to get to know you—by the way you handle him, talk to him, convey your feelings to him through touching him, (3) to provide routines and signals that help him to anticipate what is going to happen to him, and (4) to introduce the first two signs.

The Programme: Stage 1

RELATIONSHIP

Love

ACTION Your baby needs to feel your love for him by the way you hold and handle him. Stroke him, cuddle him, kiss and be very loving towards him. You cannot see his deaf/blindness or yet know how this will affect him, so enjoy him for the baby he is. Try to relax when nursing him or he will feel your tension and be uncomfortable.

WHY Children must receive affection if they are to return it—without a loving relationship with you, your baby will not want to learn to please you. It is a mother's pleasure in her child's learning that makes him want to learn more.

Smell, touch

ACTION Use a nice scent and always use it. If possible, wear clothing of the same material when you are nursing him (an overall is a simple solution).

WHY He must have things which help him recognise you if he is to form a relationship with you; you are telling him, this is 'me'.

ACTION If, because of a late start, resistance to contact has been built up, your baby may not respond to your attempts to make a relationship with him. In such cases it can help if, several times a day for short periods (4 to 5 minutes—never more than 10), you hold him firmly in your arms and ignore his resistance. Talk and sing to him, rock and jog—distract him in any way that you can but keep him close to you. If you do this regularly every day, your baby will learn to put up with it, then, as the things you are doing become familiar, he will begin to enjoy it—it becomes a playtime in which he learns to participate and, in participating, to learn. This procedure is called 'intensive play therapy' and it has been used successfully with deaf/blind children even of the age of 4 where the resistance to contact has been very strong.

COMMUNICATION

ACTION Watch out for the ways in which your baby will be beginning to communicate with you.

> First: by different ways of crying which indicate he is hungry, or uncomfortable, tired or just lonely.

> Then: notice if his behaviour changes when you touch him, or when, without touching him, you speak to him, blow on his face, let him be aware of the scent you use, i.e. does he move slightly in your direction, still and remain quiet as if waiting for something more to happen, is he comforted when you nurse him?

Respond to these communications from him by making contact, talking to him, giving him a hug and letting him feel the way your face changes when you smile at him—this way he will know you have received his message.

WHY The development of the relationship and early communication between mother and child relies on eye contact and facial expression, both of which are denied to the deaf/blind baby at this stage. We have to look for these other things that tell us he is aware of us and we have to respond to them in such a way that he knows we have responded. It is seeing her baby's smile that makes mother smile in response and then the baby responds to her smile by smiling back—its a three-way process that we have in some way also to get going with the deaf/blind child.

Listening

ACTION Talk to your baby just as if he can hear you, about himself, what you are doing to him and how you love him. Put lots of emotional tone in your voice.

WHY Because a child is deaf, it does not mean that we do not talk to him. All mums talk to their babies even though babies know no words; they learn words because we talk to them. Although a deaf/blind child may not have enough hearing to learn to speak, he can get many helpful clues from tone, from your body movements, the vibrations felt on your face and throat when you speak—and in the process will also learn a lot about you. By talking to him we are also making sure that should he have sufficient hearing for speech, he is receiving the necessary speech sounds to prepare him for this.

First two signs

ACTION When you use the word 'Mummy' or his own name, put extra emphasis on this and, as you say 'Mummy', take his hand in yours and gently tap your chest; when you say his name, take his hand and gently touch it to his own chest.

You　　　　　　　　　　　　　　　**Me**

40

WHY These are the signs for 'me' and 'you'—later on we will have special signs for 'Mummy' and for your baby's own name.

Vibration ACTION Have his head against your chest sometimes when you are talking to him so that he can be aware of the vibrations. (Try listening to someone's voice yourself in this way.)

WHY Vibration will provide clues about speech, about you, and he may be comforted by hearing your heart beat if he recognises this as part of his life before he was born.

VISION ACTION If your child is blind, when you are talking to him speak closely to his face so that he can feel the puffs of air as you speak. If you know he has some vision, it is very important that you encourage him to look at you, or at least in your direction. To do this you might:

wear very bright lipstick,
wear glasses (or frames without lenses) with silver foil round the rims,
have a bright, sparkly slide in your hair,
wear a disco headshade,
have an angle lamp which lights up your face.

WHY Observation of mother/child behaviour suggests that mothers deliberately position themselves where their baby can see them, that they hold their heads in such a way that their eyes are in a direct line with the baby's, and that the bottle is automatically held so the baby can see it, even though mothers know the baby is too young to focus and see it clearly. It is important, whether there is some vision or not, that we get the child early into the habit of looking in our direction when we are talking to him, for this is the natural way of a conversation, whichever method we may be using for conversing.

FEEDING ACTION Feeding a baby who seems always so small and helpless to begin with is an act of loving and a very moving experience for most mothers. If your baby is a poor feeder, your natural anxiety can often add to the problems. Consciously relax and try not to worry—consult your doctor or welfare clinic if you have the slightest concern over feeding: unnecessary worry is a waste of precious energy. Many deaf/blind children have feeding problems, but seem to grow up none the worse for it. If you like to be quiet when feeding, make sure you organise things so this is possible; if you prefer it to be a family affair, make the other children realise that this is a happy time for the baby and that by being there they share it.

WHY Because they are often small at birth, some of these children may need more frequent feeding for a while, but keep to a regular time, if possible, because it helps to build up his anticipation of things that happen regularly. Feeding is quite tiring for the baby and he may not be able to suck for as long as it would take to take the amount suggested for the average baby.

Signal

ACTION Touch your baby's lips gently with your finger just before you begin each feed. This is to tell him that it is time for the feed and is preparation for the sign for 'food'.

Smell

ACTION If you are feeding your baby from a bottle, hold it so that he has a chance to get the smell of the milk before you touch his lips, and then let him have the feed.

WHY Smell is evidence that there is something 'out there', and every bit of information of this kind that we can draw the baby's attention to is valuable to him.

MOVEMENT

Signal

ACTION Move him gently when taking him from place to place. Begin at once to give him a signal that he is going to be picked up and lifted into space by gently tapping his arms. When you put him down anywhere, let him feel the weight of his body on the mattress before you take your hands from under him.

WHY Before he was born, apart from some limb flexing, all the baby's movements were those of his mother—her rhythmic breathing, walking, lying down, hoovering and so on. Now he is no longer part of a moving thing, but a moving thing himself, and he cannot see where he is being moved to or what he is put down on. Rapid, unexpected movement must be very frightening, so we must help him this way to anticipate what is going to happen.

ACTION When he is awake and/or for short periods before a feed, carry him round with you in a baby sling positioned to the front of you.

WHY This will help him to experience those things which meant security to him before birth. It also provides close contact and shared movement experience which will add to knowing you and recognising you through the way you move.

ROUTINES

ACTION Try to handle your baby in the same way for each routine that occurs frequently during each day. For instance, holding your baby for feeding is different from, say, when you are dressing him or bathing him. If the way you hold him is always the same for a particular activity, he has another clue to what is going to happen.

WHY It is only by learning to recognise things that happen with monotonous regularity, and associating them with the event in which they occur, that a baby begins to make sense of and learn to anticipate daily life patterns. Seeing and hearing provide consistent information; we must provide consistency in other ways so that the deaf/blind child also develops anticipation.

Bathing

ACTION Being stripped of your warm clothing and suddenly

rubbed by a wet, soapy hand cannot be a pleasant experience, so have a warm room, warm towels and warm hands. Check the heat of the bath carefully and if your baby's feet and hands seem cold, warm them before he goes into the bath.

WHY Some 'rubella' children have heart lesions and therefore often poor circulation, so that their feet and hands are colder than the rest of their body, and water that is body heat may seem too hot to their extremities. A bad experience in bathing can put a child off his bath for some time.

ACTION Always use the bathroom for bathing and toiletting.

WHY Your baby will quickly be aware of differences in certain surroundings—if you bath and toilet him in any old place, he will be missing the clues that will help him to use the right place for these things later on.

Signal

ACTION Alert your baby to what is going to happen by having a nice-smelling soap that he can smell before the bath and a matching talc to use afterwards, or dabble his hand in the water before you actually immerse him.

Body image

ACTION When he is undressed, either before or after his bath, gently caress his body as if massaging it. Talk to him about the parts of his body as you touch them.

WHY To help him get used to being touched and to get to know your touch. It is also a way of making a relationship for you both.

ACTION Lie your baby on his tummy both during undressing and dressing and during massage routines.

WHY He needs to get used to being in this position as early as possible, in order to prevent a dislike of it which is common to children with a visual problem. Many of the exercises necessary to develop motor ability occur in this position.

Sleep

ACTION Try to create a regular sleeping pattern and provide clues that will enable your baby to identify the various parts. Timing is important—if he wakes in the night, try not to lift him, but soothe him in his cot. This is not always possible, but if there is a definite period of time when he is never lifted, it will help him recognise night time.

WHY Regular sleeping patterns are important to a baby's health—the amount of time a child sleeps varies, but if it is regular and in keeping with his needs, he will not get overtired. Children often sleep less, but can be happy at night remaining in the cot if they have some mobiles to watch. Avoid creating habits which become hard to break, e.g. taking the child into your own bed.

ACTION Do not use more than a very faint light when you attend him in the night (the light is for your benefit only). When

Signals   you put him down at night and get him up in the morning, have a very bright light in the room (from side lights directed to the ceiling to give ambient light rather than a light hanging down from the centre of the room).

WHY Light and darkness help to regulate children's sleeping patterns. There may be no difference for the child who is blind or has only partial sight, so we must make the division for him in these other ways.

ACTION During the day, sleep him in a pram or somewhere that is *not* his night-time cot, and when he wakes put him in the sling and carry him round with you. When you put him to sleep in the cot at night, wrap him firmly in his shawl or blanket to make him feel secure. When sleeping in the day in the pram, do not wrap him but lay a light covering on him and just tuck this round him.

WHY We are creating differences that will help the deaf/blind baby sort out situations which would otherwise seem similar to him because he cannot know of the environmental factors which make them different for us.

Toiletting   ACTION Before you undo the pins to take off the nappy, rub his
Nappy changing   hips gently in a downward direction. Touch his hips again just
Body awareness   before you do up the clean nappy.

Signal   WHY This is another alerting signal and it is preparation for the early toilet sign for pulling down your pants.

Dressing   ACTION Gently touch the part of the body the clothing is to go
Signals   on before putting it on, e.g. if an all-in-one garment, legs in first, just run your hand up his leg beforehand and say 'Put in your *legs*'; or if his vest over his head, run your hands down over his head to show him where to expect the clothing and say 'Over your *head*'.

WHY Helps anticipation to grow—he cannot see the clothes coming towards him. He will soon get used to being dressed and undressed and we can make the reminders less and less until he is ready to learn the names of his clothing.

PLAY   ACTION Your baby is too young for play in the real sense, but whenever you are nursing him and talking to him, hold his hands, caress them, pat them and, if he is able to open them, rub the palms. He will not be in control of the movements of his hands but he will probably grasp your finger and you can encourage this.

WHY Your baby's hands (together with your own) will be his main learning tool later on. He must learn to tolerate having his hands touched and moved as early as possible.

ACTION Like all babies, your deaf/blind baby will enjoy being

44

rocked. It is believed to be good for them, helping circulation and respiration, muscle tone and digestion, and it often comforts the child in moments of stress. For these reasons, we should consider rocking as part of our play with the baby. It can become a habit that stands in the way of learning with some visually disabled children, but so long as we provide lots of other interesting experiences as well, as he gets older, we should avoid this happening.

Stage 2

INTRODUCTION

I hope that by using the ideas in Stage 1 you are beginning to see the kind of information your baby needs and the way in which you can provide it. His daily routines are no different from any other baby's, just more carefully planned. In Stage 2 we shall continue in the same way, but bringing more things to the baby's attention (and they must be things which affect him personally) and watching for more clues from him that tell us he is becoming aware of these things.

First a few comments about this time in your baby's life. It is often a time, just when we are beginning to feel that things are settling down, when we are faced with hospital visits or admissions. This upsets all our nicely planned routines and the child himself. If your baby goes into hospital, try to go with him so that at least the relationship with the person he knows best is disturbed as little as possible. Sometimes a different environment can bring about changes which are advantageous and one should try to gain something positive, as well as the obvious medical benefit. You have to learn to take these things in your stride; the earlier things that can be put right are put right, the greater will be the benefit to the child.

It is also a time when your baby would be expected to begin to take his first solid food. This is sometimes a difficult time for deaf/blind children and I have covered it in detail. However, I hope that you will be lucky and be able to introduce solids to a baby who thoroughly enjoys them, and then you can ignore this part of the programme.

In Stage 1 we began communication with the use of two signs—'you' and 'me'. We also began using 'signals' to alert the baby to what was going to happen to him, e.g. connecting the smell of his milk with feeding time. We use these signals until such time as we know the baby understands what they mean, then we can substitute the proper signs—but this is some way off yet. Some of the 'signals' are also natural gestures that we all use, either when we are speaking or as a substitute for speech, e.g. waving your hand=goodbye, or raking your fingers through your hair=comb. Often the real sign is similar to the signal, but the child needs to go through the stage of signalling (or non-verbal communication if we were speaking of a seeing/hearing child) as it alerts him to something which is part of or more general to an event, rather than too specific. From the signals we build up to general signs and from the more general signs to the specific, e.g. from just touching the baby's lips before his bottle (a signal), we advance to the sign for 'food' meaning all kinds of food, and then later he will learn the signs for each kind of food. As we work through the six stages of the programme there will be new signs and signals, together with signs for the signals used at a previous stage. We will begin gradually but increase the number with every stage.

Communication will always be the most important part of any programme for a deaf/blind child, but movement is also important, for the actual act of communicating is, of course, movement, whatever form this takes. So we need now to begin to encourage the development of motor skills—not only for communication, but because movement allows the exploration by which the baby will gather information from us and for himself later on. The early reflex movements will now be lessening and the baby will start to make movement which, random at first, will soon be made deliberately. Normally a baby's first responses are to being touched or touching something. Then what he sees encourages him to reach and touch for himself, to grasp it, and then he learns to move to see, touch or grasp something he hears. If he lacks, or has poor, vision and hearing, the incentive to respond by moving is also likely to be poor—so finding ways of encouraging him to move must now become an integral part of the programme. In addition, we must make him aware of his own body and the movements he can make with his various limbs as these gradually come under his control. And as he uses his growing ability to move, we must observe this, for it will tell us a great deal about how he feels, what he can do and, above all, what he is telling us. Should you at any time have doubts about using the ideas suggested for motor development, **please** consult your doctor or your child's physiotherapist.

It is suggested that initially a child may have difficulty in attending to more than one source of stimulation at a time—that first he notices things by touch, then by vision, and that only as he becomes less bound to vision does he begin to listen. As the nervous system matures, he learns to integrate all these sources of information and to use them altogether. Very often the deaf/blind child who has a little vision does seem to become impelled to use this and even though we might suspect he hears sounds, he seems to ignore them. We would expect no more than a stilling or startle to sounds that were not connected to anything he could touch or see dimly, e.g. the door banging, water running, the car starting up etc., but even these are often completely ignored. This inconsistency makes it very difficult to estimate whether or not there is useful residual hearing, but you must keep talking and feeding in those sounds which are likely to be meaningful and attract his attention, otherwise he may lose interest in listening and never use to best advantage that which/he does possess.

As you move around the house, train yourself to notice those visual clues which you think your child might be able to see, smells he could be helped to become aware of, sounds and vibrations which could mean something to him (light from the window, talcum powder, footsteps as you approach him). Try getting around the house with your eyes closed: what are the things that you feel help you identify different places? Go round with bare feet: would the different surfaces tell you where you were?

These days most fathers participate in the early care of their children and this now becomes important for your baby, for whom the father can become a very positive person with his own special place in the routine of the day. There should be some activity that only he does with the baby—usually movement such as jogging up and down—and a physical feature that the baby can learn to recognise as belonging only to him. Unless you are both the same height, your baby will probably become aware of the difference in the height to which he is lifted when either of you pick him up or handle him.

Give your baby time to accept the new and to learn to recognise its meaning and effect on him. Do not expect immediate responses; keep the input going and when he has absorbed enough information and is developmentally ready, he will respond. Remember, everything must be pleasant and enjoyed by you both—if you are happy and enjoying things, he will catch the spirit of it from you. It is never all that easy, but try, for it will help you both. Remember to pass on the necessary information and techniques to any person helping you so that there is consistency of handling.

The Programme: Stage 2

RELATIONSHIP

ACTION On the assumption that your baby now knows 'you are there', he next needs to learn what you are like, to notice other things about you besides scent and handling. Take his hand(s) over your face so that he can feel those features (hair, eyes etc.) which make you 'you'. Put his hand(s) on your face, lips or throat when you speak, sing to him, or when you laugh with him. If you are having fun and you are talking and smiling at him, your voice and its vibrations will also convey the loving you want him to feel and return.

WHY He has to build up first a 'picture' of you and then of others with which to compare the 'picture' he comes to have of himself (with our help) and so to become aware of his own identity as a person separate from all others.

ACTION Wear a brooch or tactile clue that you touch with the child's hand as you pick him up (or stop to talk to him) and, having touched it this way, immediately touch the baby's hand to your chest. If he has some vision, you can use a brightly coloured object, but he still must touch it.

Decide upon something which will enable your baby to make a similar connection with Daddy—a beard or moustache is perfect, or a tiepin or lapel badge, so long as it is completely different from the object Mummy uses. Show your baby how to touch it and feel it, then touch his hand to Daddy's chest.

WHY Everything we can use to make our baby aware of us and of the things that distinguish us, helps him to build up a relationship with us.

COMMUNICATION

From baby to you

ACTION Observe if your baby's way of communicating is changing. Can you pick out the difference between a hungry and a discomfort cry? Is he making sounds other than crying—happy sounds? Does he make body movements to tell you something—wriggling if he is uncomfortable, sort of excited little movements when he is happy and so on? If you think he 'knows' you, what does he do that makes you think this? These are all ways in which your baby is communicating with you. If you think he is hungry, you will automatically meet this need, but somehow you must make your baby aware that it was because *he* communicated the need to you, *you* provided the drink. Otherwise he may not realise it was the sound he made that got him the drink or he may just think he communicated with the bottle! Vision and hearing provide the link in the ordinary way—it is a very vital link. If, for instance, the cry is a hungry one, pick your baby up and take him with you and hold him or have him close while you prepare the food/drink; telling him, the same as you would a hearing child, that it won't be long—think how much more related action there is than if he was left to lie with no information while you totally vanished.

Observe if your baby is beginning to recognise any of the signals you have been giving him, e.g. is there any movement of his arms up towards you when you give him the signal for being picked up, or similar body movements in dressing and undressing?

WHY If we are not aware of the baby's efforts to 'tell' and we do not let him know we are aware because we are not sure how to decipher the message or have to work on a trial and error method, he will not be stimulated to keep at it.

Signal

ACTION When he shows you he is pleased you have, for example, given him some food, or changed his nappy, and he is saying 'thank you' in his own way, give him the 'good boy' signal—a little pat on the head. Use this at all times to signal your pleasure in something he has done.

From you to baby

New signs

Mealtimes

ACTION A mother does not talk to her baby in single words, she uses simple sentences with emphasis on the important word. She does not expect him to use words for a long time, and when he does she will accept single words or even half-formed words to begin with. Sign simple sentences to the deaf/blind baby, saying them at the same time with emphasis on the important words. Take your baby's hand (fist probably) and say/sign as follows. 'Are you hungry?' Touch his hand to his chest (=you) then rub it in a circular movement on his tummy (=hungry).

'Here's your food/drink.' Touch his hand to his bottle so he knows it is there, then touch it to his chest (=your) and to his mouth (=eat/drink).

Bedtime

'Time for you to sleep.' Touch his hand to his chest (=you) and then to the side of his head (=sleep), the side on which you are going to lay him.

Bath time

'It's bath time.' Touch his hand to his chest (=you) and then rub it gently down his chest from his neck several times (=bath).

These signs must be given as near the actual event as possible or they will not become associated with the right thing.

WHY Self-explanatory.

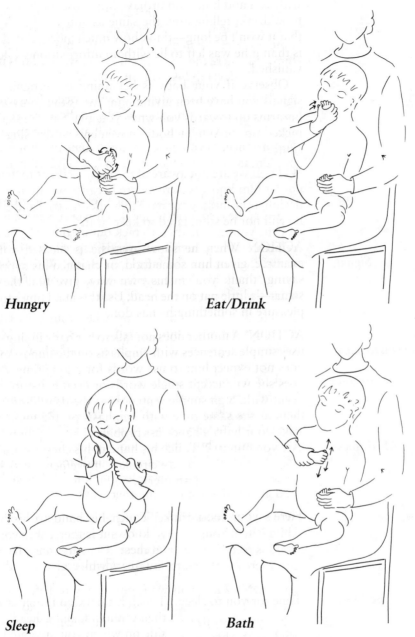

Hungry   **Eat/Drink**

Sleep   **Bath**

LISTENING   ACTION Observe and make a note of the awareness your baby
shows of environmental sounds, e.g. doors banging, telephone
bell, hoover, music, voices, or any noise-making toys you might
sound close to him. Observe how he responds: does he stop what
he is doing, turn his head slightly, still his eyes or his body, does he
adopt a whole body position that suggests he might be listening?
Is he aware of you approaching him if you are talking to him at
the same time? At what distance does he first appear to be aware
of your voice?

51

WHY Observations of this kind are useful to audiologists who will be trying to estimate how much hearing your baby has from time to time. It will also help you to know what *sounds* interest him and where these sounds must be; we need this information if we are to develop his skills in listening.

ACTION In routine situations which occur frequently, try to use some very specific phrases—similar to those we are using with the signs and to which later on we will attach the appropriate signs. For instance, as you pick him up: '*Come* to Mummy.'; when you put him in his cot: '*Down* you go.'; when Daddy takes him from Mummy '*Go* to Daddy.'

WHY The child who has some useful hearing must hear speech sounds if he is to learn to speak. However, speech is too complex for the young deaf child to pick out all the component parts and remember the sequence of sounds, especially if he is without the visual clues of lips and facial expression. With regular use, these phrases help him to recognise the key words for which he will learn the appropriate true signs later on.

ACTION This may be the time when your baby is issued with a hearing aid if this is thought to be of help to him. Make sure that when you put it on each time the sounds he hears are pleasant—a loving greeting from you, a song he enjoys hearing you sing and is rocked to, or any sound that he has shown he likes. Follow carefully the instructions given to you on the use and setting of the aids. If the child objects, you can try to get him used to wearing the earmoulds only to begin with, but give him time to become accustomed to both the aid and a change in the sounds he hears. It may be that he will hear some sounds for the first time and be a little afraid of them—try to let him know what makes the sound and get his interest in it in other ways.

WHY A hearing aid only amplifies sound, it does not make a child listen. Sounds have to be interesting and have meaning if a child is to remember and recognise them: *we* have to encourage his interest and create situations which give sounds meaning.

ACTION When you want your baby to listen, make sure you have as little background noise as possible (no radio or TV on when you are talking to him). If you find it helps, raise your voice slightly (higher pitch), but on no account shout.

WHY When we are listening we are able to cut out those sounds to which we do not wish to pay attention—the deaf child may not be able to do this until such time as he is aware of those things which have meaning for him.

ACTION Before you speak to your baby get into the habit of alerting him—a little touch on his shoulder and a word such as 'Hi' or perhaps his name.

WHY It is easy if you are deaf to miss the first word or two of something being said to you unless the speaker has first made it quite clear that he is going to speak to you. If you are deaf/blind, without these alerting signals you might not even be aware there was anyone there who could speak to you. Getting the child's attention to what you are doing or saying/signing is vital when he is a little bit older, so get started now.

ACTION Babies generally love being held against one's shoulder; this is a good position to talk to your baby when his aid is not on, because you can turn your head and speak very close to one of his ears (if there is a better one, hold him so that this is the one you speak into). Watch to see if there is any change in your baby's behaviour if you speak for a minute or so and then stop; does he move closer or even turn a little? If he appears not to like it, he has certainly told you he was aware of something—and we must always remember that a negative response is still a response.

VOCALISING

ACTION Your baby may begin to make new sounds now. Every now and then take a short tape recording of them, noting date and time.

WHY It will provide a record to show if the range is increasing and whether he is beginning to repeat sounds, e.g. babbling.

ACTION Copy the vowel sounds your baby makes and watch his reactions to see if he has heard you make them. The next stage will be to encourage him to repeat them when he has heard your imitation of his sounds; it is probably too early, but if he can give it back, encourge the turn taking.

WHY Turn taking is the basis of conversation and social interaction, a vital stage in learning to communicate. Give your baby plenty of time to organise his response before you offer him another sample of the sound he made.

PLAY

Your baby will begin to be awake for longer periods now. Some of this time should be spent interacting with a person and some on his own in his pram. Play provides lots of opportunity for encouraging a baby to learn to use his vision and hearing and to help him practise his motor skills. While you must bear in mind the need to make play a learning experience, for you both it has always to be a lot of fun which you have *together*, cementing the relationship which began in Stage 1.

With a person

ACTION Sing and move together. Rock to the rhythm of a tune. Dance to various rhythms with your baby in your arms. Romp with him—jump and hop with him in your arms, jog him up and down on your knees, rock with him in a rocking chair, lie on the floor with him rocking gently from side to side.

WHY Deaf/blind children need to be introduced to movement through us. We each have our own way of moving and so he will also be getting clues which help to identify us for him.

Specific phrase

ACTION Talk to him about what you are doing: if, say, you are turning round and round with him, say 'Round and round and round—stop', and make sure you stop exactly as you say 'stop';

wait a while and then repeat. The gap is important. It gives the child a chance (if he likes what you are doing) to try to ask you to do it again. Watch for any kind of small body movement which could just be a signal for 'more' and, if it is there, respond at once by doing the activity again. Once the child realises he is in command of the situation and can get what he wants this way, he has made a big step forward. It is vital that you should watch for these 'signals' from the child to you and that sometimes you use

Specific phrase

the child's own signals on him saying 'You want some *more*', so that the child knows not only do you understand his message but you can send the same message to him.

WHY The child's first attempts at communication are often so fleeting that they are easily missed; if we miss them, he may stop trying.

Rhymes

ACTION With the child sitting on your lap, his back firmly against you, play a simple nursery rhyme with actions. I would suggest 'Two little dickie birds sitting on a wall' and you can find this and other action rhymes in the *Ladybird Finger Play* book or Rostron's *Finger Play for Nursery Schools*. If you speak it rhythmically, your movements will also be rhythmic. Do it two or three times at the most, but do it every day. Use only this one rhyme during this stage. Do it 'hands on', of course, and observe whether the child is beginning to recognise the sequence of movement and through your hands you can feel him beginning to anticipate some of it.

WHY Simple patterns of movement and sound help to develop the ability to remember sequences and are a preparation for participation (joining in with you) and later for imitation (by himself).

ACTION An alternative lap game which stresses the action the child is making is to sit with him on your lap as above and gently move his arms up/down, in to the midline/out; bring his hands together and bring them to his face. Make up a little sequence of these and do them in the same order each time and saying 'up, down' etc.

Play on the floor
Signal

ACTION Have a special floor rug or blanket for use for play periods—being put on this acts as a signal to the baby for what follows once he has got used to the activities which are always in this particular place. Choose a good texture, a bright colour and not less than 4 ft square because later we shall want to encourage the baby to move about on it. The following ideas are some which you can use when the baby is on his play rug.

ACTION Join your baby on the rug and lie quietly beside him. Do not stimulate him, but notice if he is aware you are there, and respond to any approach he might make to you. Observe how he plays and moves: does he like rubbing things or rubbing himself, or does he seem interested in light sources, or does he appear to be listening?

54

WHY The baby himself is the best source of information and if we begin with what interests him, if we can join in what he does, it is more likely we can lead him from there to the things we want him to be interested in and encourage him to join in.

ACTION Play tickling games with him such as 'Round and round the garden' and 'This little piggie'.

WHY We are not using these rhymes to encourage him to move because it is we who are making the movements. Here we are creating an opportunity for anticipating a climax. We are beginning an input of sounds, words and touching various parts of the baby's body in turn, first slowly, then gradually building up in speed, loudness and nearness to the child. You can make up lots of little sequences like this to play on the floor or after his bath when his body is bare (e.g. blowing raspberries).

ACTION Play a game of putting your hands over your baby's eyes and then releasing them, or put a paper hankie over his face, then remove it—if he is physically able, he may do this for himself or you can show him how to do it. This game has to be fun; give him lots of praise when he manages to do it for himself. Put the hankie over your own face and show him it is there and help him to pull it off.

WHY This is a preliminary to learning that things remain in existence even when they are out of sight or cannot be touched (object permanence).

Body awareness

ACTION Play with his bare feet and his hands, rubbing and patting them, rubbing them with different textures, blowing on them. Tie little bells or pompoms on his feet and wrists for short periods.

MOTOR DEVELOPMENT

ACTION With the child on his back on the rug, encourage him to turn his head from the midline to one side and then from the midline to the other side. Use a torch to encourage him to move this way, also a sound at the side we want him to turn and a puff of air on his cheek—if he does not do it of his own accord, gently prompt him and show him how pleased you are when he manages it.

WHY The ability to control the movements of one's body develops from head down through the body and to the extremities. Therefore, since he may lack the incentive to do this of his own accord because the world is not sufficiently visually exciting, we must help him to achieve this first step towards being able to move from one position to another, i.e., rolling. Remember, however much we may encourage a child to move, he will not be able to do it for himself until the nerves and muscles have progressed to the appropriate stage (this is called maturation). A baby sits because he has grown to the sitting stage, but *also* because we have given him lots of sitting experience on our laps or propped up somewhere well supported.

Rolling

ACTION When he can move his head freely, you can begin to encourage him to roll to either side from his back—the head turn is followed by the body move and you can gently prompt this to begin with. Three ways are suggested for doing this.

1. If the baby will grasp a ring with his left hand, pull this gently to bring him to his right side and vice versa.

2. Touch his shoulder, extending the underneath arm in the direction of the roll, holding the other one up and moving in the rolling direction.

3. If your baby has sufficient vision to see a bright scarf round your neck, encourage him to hold and pull on it to roll.

Head control

ACTION Lie your baby on his tummy with a small rolled-up towel under his chest and arms (so his arms hang over it and he can feel the floor). Encourage him to lift his head to look at a torchlight or a bright toy. Lie in front of your baby so you are face to face, or lie with him on your chest face to face and encourage him to lift his head by blowing gently on his face, talking, singing or smiling at him.

WHY These actions help to strengthen head control and neck muscle tone and are also the first stage of crawling.

ACTION If you have had a late start in the programme and your little one has already acquired a dislike of being on his tummy, get him used to the position with you and do it gradually. Sit with him held towards your chest and gradually lie down with him, getting a bit nearer to supine each week until you are completely lying down with him and he is familiar with the experience through sharing it with you. (Make sure you have a good prop for your back as you go through this process.)

ACTION When your baby is able to lift his head quite strongly when prone, bring his arms forward over the roll of towel and show him how to take a little weight upon them.

WHY Pre-crawling activity.

ACTION Put a foam roll under the baby's chest which is big enough to allow him to be resting on his hands and knees, then roll him back and forth very gently so that his hands take a little of his weight when they are on the floor.

WHY Pre-crawling exercise.

ACTION Sit him cross legged on the floor and encourage him to lean forward and take some weight on his hands; do not leave him to do this without support or leave him alone, rather do it with him placed between your legs as you sit on the floor. Sitting in this position between your legs (but not leaning foward) or sitting on your lap, rock him gently from side to side, allowing him to correct his balance to keep upright.

WHY Being able to balance your body sideways and forwards by taking your weight on your hands is necessary to being able to sit alone.

ACTION With his knees bent and his feet against a hard surface (a board or book), encourage him to stretch out his legs and push this away.

Motor development and body awareness

ACTION With the baby lying on his back, put a small object on his chest, e.g. a little herb bag (nice smell) or a small toy that vibrates, and show him how to bring both his hands to the midline and touch the object. Then place the object to the left of his chest and locate with his left hand, then to the right and using his right hand. If you put a small firm cushion under his lower neck and shoulder, it will help to relax his shoulders and bring his arms forward.

WHY Everything we can do to show him how he can move helps him.

Grasp

ACTION The next stage in the development of the use of his arms and hands is for him to learn to grasp. A child with normal vision has watched his own hands moving and seen them knock up against toys etc. that we have put there or held there and he is encouraged this way to grasp. Where vision is restricted we may have actually to put something, say a ring, into the child's hand and show him how to grasp it, alerting him to its presence by holding it against his hand and giving him prompting until he has learned to grasp it for himself. This must be done with either hand and leads up to learning to grasp with both hands together and bringing the object up towards his face. Help to direct his hands by holding his elbows.

WHY These are all recognised small sequential steps through which all children pass in learning to control the use of their hands and learning to co-ordinate this with the use of their vision. Unless we make the children aware of what there is there to be grasped and played with, deaf/blind babies may be delayed in the use of their hands or may merely develop stereotype hand movement. It is vital that they develop hand skills, for their hands will be a major source of information.

Search

ACTION Now comes the need to show the child how to search and follow things and grasp them in order to bring them to his mouth—the mouth is a source of information to all babies and it may remain so for a deaf/blind child much longer than for the child with normal vision. Here you touch the object to baby's hand, move it a little way away, showing baby how to move his hand to find it. A light on the toy or use of a noise-making toy if he has shown that he hears this, can help baby to achieve this stage. (Two people can play this game with baby, one nursing and showing him, 'hands on', what to do, the other holding the toy.)

57

Lots of excited praise when he succeeds helps to make him want to keep trying.

VISION

ACTION Now is the time to begin propping your baby up a little when he is awake—the small pillow to begin with, increasing this gradually by the addition of about a nappy-thickness at a time until the child is almost sitting up. If head control is poor, support at each side.

WHY It is very important that your baby is in a position where he can receive the best visual stimulation and information as near the normal time as possible. If he is blind, he will find little to reach out for when lying on his back. Just as, in order to hear, you have first to learn to listen, in order to use your vision to see, you have first to learn to look. When you have learned to look, you then have to learn to use both eyes together, to track moving objects, to be able to focus so that you can see things at different distances, to be able to look quickly from one thing to another and to scan a wide field to seek out what you want to see (later for reading). In addition you have to learn to do these things while moving as well as when still. Routines and play provide lots of opportunity for developing these skills which, if the child can learn them, will enable him to make the best use of any vision he may have.

Eye contact

ACTION The most important 'thing' a child has to learn to look at is his mother. Watch where he seems best able to suggest to you that he sees something and try to get your eyes in line with his. Draw his attention to your face in any way that you can—coloured sticky tape on your eyebrows, a matchbox on your nose—and always sit where the light is on your face and hair. (Seeing babies are known to study their mothers' hairline and to respond to a pattern which is facelike.) If you have a child who tends to avoid eye contact, you will certainly know when you get it; it is quite a wonderful moment when you really know your child is seeing you, however briefly. It is the moment to smile and say 'hallo' with real meaning. Hold a bright cover in front of your face and, when the child is looking at it, move it away so that he is then looking at your face.

Hand awareness

ACTION The next important thing for him to learn to look at is hands—yours and his own. Wear very bright nail polish, put 'thimbles' made of shiny material on the tops of your fingers, stick brightly coloured sticky tape on your hands or wear very bright and various textured gloves. Put similar things on his hands to make him aware of his own movements—and later on his feet and other parts of his limbs for the same reason.

WHY To learn about your hands, about his own hands and what he can do by moving them and using them as tools.

ACTION Observe what kind of things attract your baby's visual attention and where he sees these best, then, when he is sitting or lying on his floor rug or in his pram during the day, put up bright shiny mobiles or balloons which move and glint for him to watch. It may be necessary to direct some light at these, but make sure the source cannot be seen by him or he will look at this and not at the mobiles. Move him round so that he is not always looking at these things from the same side. Other ideas are a lampshade with fairy lights round it, bright shapes stuck on a fairly dark wall, shine a torch on the wall or, if you have an overhead projector, throw bright pictures on to the wall. These will be better in a dark or dimly lit room. Which objects provide the most opportunity for your baby to fixate on only you can tell by your careful observation; make your own choice as to which you use.

WHY Vision develops by being used; if we do not stimulate the deaf/blind child who does have some vision, it may never become as efficient as it could.

ACTION If your baby does fixate on a bright spot on the wall, move it along a little way very slowly and watch to see if he follows it by turning his head.

WHY This is the beginning of tracking—a skill we shall be working on through the next two stages.

Multisensory   ACTION When your baby is in his pram and playing by himself, tie things around it, bright, noisy and well-textured things for him to see and feel and knock against as he moves. You can use pram toys that are strung across the pram and fix these so that he can touch them, not only with his hands, but also with his feet. When he is on the floor rug, the same kind of incidental experience can be made available to him if you make the kind of apparatus illustrated below. Change the things on it so that he has new experiences as well as the familiar. Observe whether when he has touched something he tries to do the same thing again. Are there some things he does not like? What do these have in common, if anything?

WHY He needs to be able to find out some things for himself and, by observing him in this situation, we shall find out through which medium he learns best.

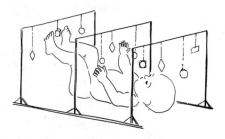

ROUTINES   ACTION Unless there is any physical reason which prevents it,
Feeding   begin very *gradually* to introduce solids, e.g. very thin baby cereals or fruits and soups which are available in tins.

WHY If children cannot see the new food or be told how nice it is (or shown that we like eating too), no wonder some of them jib at finding food of a strange texture and taste in their mouths. The older a child gets, the more sensitive he becomes to these differences, so it is important to begin as near normal time for weaning as possible.

ACTION Use a plastic spoon and encourage the baby to feel it before you begin feeding him. Warm the food. Initially, only offer him one small teaspoonful before his liquid feed at the meal time he is usually most hungry. Touch his lips with the spoon and wait for him to open his mouth. Give him a chance to smell the food. Touch his tongue with the spoon several times before emptying the spoon to remind him to swallow. If he is reluctant to open his mouth, try rubbing his cheek back and forth or rubbing his lips gently with your fingertips on which there is a drop of milk. If he dislikes any of the foods, is it the taste or does the smell warn him before he has tasted it? It helps to know this should it be necessary to do a little camouflaging.

WHY Feeding must continue to be a pleasant time. At this stage we are more concerned to get your baby used to these new experiences than to fill him with solids. At the same time we must be firm, and once we have introduced one spoonful at this particular meal, we must keep to it until he has got used to it and accepts it.

ACTION When he is happy to take the one spoonful, increase it to two spoonfuls at the beginning of the feed. And now offer one spoonful of *milk* before the bottle at other feeds. Continue to increase the number of spoonfuls gradually, add more flavours and textures and use at other mealtimes as well—until weaning is completed. Take your time over this, but keep at it. Get all the things you need by you before starting; nothing upsets a deaf/blind baby more than having to stop in the middle of feeding, particularly as it would be difficult to make him understand why this was necessary.

ACTION If your baby has a bottle, help him to put his hands on it when feeding; if he finds it too slippery, put a cover on it.

WHY Beginning of self-help and knowing where the food comes from.

ACTION Put his hands on such things as rusks, biscuits or dry toast—not for him to eat, but to get used to their feel so he is less likely to refuse to hold them later on.

Bathing ACTION Bath time is full of interesting things, all of which impinge on the child himself and affect him in some way. Begin to use the real sign for 'bathing' (see under Communication) just before you undress him and again just before you put him in the bath. Soap his tummy, then take his hand and gently rub it *up and down* it (the same movement as the sign for bath). Put his hand on

60

the talc tin and let him feel you shake it—remember to let him smell this and the soap.

WHY Because the bathing routine has been in the same sequence each time, your baby should be beginning to anticipate some of the things that occur and to recognise some of the things that are used; he should be building up a picture made of separate things which are beginning to join together and make a whole event which he understands and can enjoy—and in which he will soon be able to participate.

Touch and being touched

ACTION When your baby is undressed—before or after his bath, depending on which you feel is best—spend a little time stroking, patting, tickling and ruffling him; rub his body with materials of different textures, e.g. silk, wool, fur, the baby hairbrush, cotton wool, tissue paper etc., not all on the same day, just a selection! You can also rub his body with such things as shaving cream, baby oil, hand cream—things which will feel different because they are of different consistencies, and wet as opposed to the dry materials. Talk to him all the time about what you are doing and what these things feel like *and* what fun it all is.

WHY The readiness to accept different tactile experiences is an asset to the deaf/blind child who often develops a dislike of touching things. If we have always given a baby these kinds of experiences, we hope he will not develop this sensitivity.

ACTION Continue the massaging—it could now be a regular massage programme (such as that advocated by Leboyer in his book *Loving Hands*.) Name the body parts as you massage them.

Undressing and dressing

ACTION Talk about each item of clothing, which part of the body it is for, whether it is going to be put on or taken off, or the type of action needed.
Tap his leg, saying:
    'Put *on* your sock/shoe.' 'Take *off* your sock/shoe.'
Tap his arm, saying:
    '*Push* your arm in the sleeve.' '*Pull* your arm out of the sleeve.'
Tap his head to remind him 'head up', saying:
    '*Pull on* your vest/jumper.' '*Pull off* your vest/jumper.'
You can also let him feel the different textures of his clothes by putting his hand on them and drawing attention to the differences.

ACTION Preparation for only.

Toiletting

When you have your baby on your lap after bathing, slip a nappy over the potty, put the potty between your legs and gently rest him on it for a few minutes. It will feel different from your lap, but if you hug and cuddle him he should not mind it just briefly. Do this every bathtime at the same time during the routine. If he accepts it, increase the time gradually to a minute or thereabouts.

WHY If your baby has had experiences which get him used to sitting on the potty before he is ready to use it, he will be less likely to object to using it when the time for this comes.

Stage 3

INTRODUCTION

Much of what we have been doing so far has been *to* the baby. Now we shall be moving towards doing more things *with* him, showing him what he can do with our help. We want to encourage him to become an 'acting' person rather than remaining passive and accepting. From being touched by us and by things, we want to help him learn to reach out and touch for himself, to grasp and to hold things and begin to explore them for information.

A second goal must be to progress to sitting with good balance and starting to creep and crawl. By the time your baby is ready to move off by himself, you must have helped him to have a greater awareness of what is around him and to want to explore. Moving out into space that has no form is not a very inviting prospect, so we must begin to prepare him—hence a new heading under 'Experience' which I have called 'Environmental'. By this I mean making him aware of things which are in his immediate home environment so that when he does crawl, some of the things he meets will have a familiar feel or look or smell: if the kitchen now becomes the place of lots of nice smells and tastes, the stairs become up and down things, or rooms can be recognised by their different floor coverings or their purpose by the objects in them, these are all useful clues which we can begin to give the child.

With longer periods awake, play now fills a larger part of his day and this means you must spend more time with him, for the deaf/blind child needs to be shown how to play, how to play in such a way that in addition to the fun of it, it is a learning experience. If you can set aside regular short periods each day when you play with him and each period is devoted to a separate aspect of play, it would be best. If you have a family it is not easy to do this, but in these early days it is only from the recognition of the pattern of daily events that life begins to make sense for the deaf/blind child and he begins to have a concept of time. Once the day has form and we can attach a signal or sign to the events in it that have meaning for the child, we can use these signals or signs to show him what to expect and, by the same token, introduce changes.

62

Because of these extra demands on your time and energy, this is the point when you should seek the help of others in stimulating your baby. Through any of the associations for the handicapped (see the list in Appendix 4), a Church group, the Red Cross or other women's groups, relations or friends, you should be able to find some 'interveners' to help you. You must be careful to explain to them your baby's special needs, his programme and ways of handling, signalling and signing to him, and you must stress the importance of consistency. Your interveners need to sit and play spontaneously with your baby to make a relationship with him before actually taking over any of the special play periods. Once such a person is happy with your baby and he is happy with her/him, take advantage of the opportunity to spend extra time with the other children in the family and to get out and socialise.

You will notice that I have not changed the bedtime routine at all since Stage 1. This should remain as uncluttered as possible. If all the preparation for bedtime can be done in the bathroom and if before this the 'goodnights' have been said so that the child does not need to go back into the family group, then going straight to his bedroom and bed sets the pattern for going to sleep. Even when a child is upset or not well, it is better if he can remain in his bedroom. Mummy should stay with him or near him if necessary, but if the bedroom represents 'sleep' and nothing else, it does help him to get the message. Comfort and love are necessary at all times, but bedtime is also a time for quiet and relaxation. I have known too many sleepless little deaf/blind beings who, often for the sake of others in the household, have been taken back to the stimulating environment of the family, remained awake the whole evening and never acquired a good sleeping pattern until they have started school. A baby who has been well occupied during the day should be ready to sleep at bedtime. Having said that, some deaf/blind children are notoriously poor sleepers during the early years, but generally happy to lie awake in their cots amusing themselves for quite long periods—if yours is like this, do your best to keep as near to your planned routine as possible as often as possible.

Some new signs, signals and phrases will now come into use and you will be encouraging the next stages in using sight, listening and vocalising. Your baby may advance more quickly in some areas than others; if so, you must move on where necessary and devote a little more time to those where there is any delay. Give your baby plenty of time to become familiar with new things: do not pressurise him, rather let him dictate the pace and show you when he is ready for more—you should by now be becoming an expert observer.

As he grows in awareness, your baby will become more and more demanding, and there will be times when you will feel frustrated and torn between the feeling that you ought to be playing with him and the fact that there are dozens of other things to be done. Do the other things. If you play with him feeling this way, it will not be successful. One mother I knew would always shut herself in the bathroom at such times and say all the 'naughty' words she knew—after that she felt better and could cope! Find a way of releasing your tension and try not to let it come between you and your baby.

RELATIONSHIP   ACTION Your baby should by now be recognising his Mummy and Daddy by those special things to which we have drawn his attention, and in some ways of his own no doubt (e.g. the difference in the vibrations of people's footsteps). Now it is time to widen his circle of people he recognises and so we must find ways of identifying other members of the family or other people coming into regular daily contact with him. Preferably this should be a tactile clue plus some special way of greeting—a kiss in a special place, being jumped up or moved in a special way, and so on.

WHY Although he would come to recognise people without help in his own good time, this would be a much slower process without the clues. When he has reached the stage of understanding that people and things have names, these names are given together with the tactile clue and will eventually take its place. If we left it to the child to use his own clues, we should not have something with which to link the name.

Signals   ACTION Now is the time to begin involving other children in the family—let them choose their special clue for the deaf/blind baby and, unless they are very young, have some special task to do (getting all the things ready for bathtime or choosing the toys for a certain activity) which is related to the care of the baby. Explain to them why it is necessary to do things in special ways so that they in turn can be knowledgeable when they talk to their friends and can feel pride when the baby progresses.

WHY To be successful, helping the deaf/blind child should be a family affair, a partnership in caring and sharing. Your attitude towards the disabled child will influence the way the other children see him and react to him. He must *not* become the centre of the family, but one of the family—as they are involved with him, so must he, in time, become involved with them.

Discipline   ACTION A good relationship with your baby allows you to exercise control over him for his own good as well as to provide him with security and affection. Although as yet the occasions will be few, they will increase as he becomes more mobile, so it is not too soon to be introducing the sign plus a firmly spoken 'No' when necessary.

New sign   WHY 'No' is often the first word a seeing/hearing child says, so it is natural to introduce it early. Explaining to a deaf/blind child why he should not do such and such a thing before he has good communication is the most difficult thing in the world and can give rise to great frustration on both sides—if 'No' and its meaning are well established in the early days, perhaps it will help.

COMMUNICATION

ACTION Begin to think of communicating with your baby not only in the context of exchanging messages—in every single activity you share you are communicating some kind of information to him. It is important to think of it in this broader way, because instead of asking yourself the question 'Am I doing this correctly?', you ask yourself the much more vital one 'Am I communicating the information that enables him to understand what I am doing and why?'

WHY Because the information a baby normally gets *for himself* from seeing and hearing has to reach the deaf/blind child *through us*.

Four new signs

ACTION Introduce, when opportunity occurs, the following new signs.

No: with the palm facing outward, move the baby's hand sharply sideways in front of his face.

Drink: hand shaped as if holding a cup moving upwards to touch thumb to corner of the baby's mouth, signing the sentence 'You (want) drink'.

Play: with palms of hands upwards make a circular movement inward/outwards several times.

Hallo: with the palm outwards make an inward/outward semi-circle at shoulder height.

No

Drink

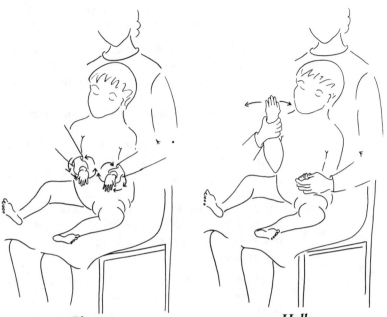

Play   *Hallo*

WHY The reason for using 'No' is given above under Discipline. Now that weaning is proceeding, we can separate food and drink; the sign which we have previously used to indicate all the foods or drinks the baby had now becomes the sign for everything he eats, and we use the above sign for 'drink' for all the kinds of liquid that he has. Play becomes an important event several times each day, and thus provides frequent opportunity to use the correct sign—once you have begun to use it, always use it just before you begin each play period so that it also becomes the signal for what is going to happen. 'Hallo' is a greeting everyone should use to let the baby know they are there: to begin with, you will hold his hand in the right position against that of the person who is greeting him; that person obviously uses the hand opposite to that the baby is using (or they would not match) and makes the movement taking the baby's hand with his. Later on, when the baby is used to this greeting, it should be sufficient for the person greeting the baby to place his palm against the baby's and move together.

ACTION   Use the following phrases with the signs.

Sign for 'No':   Say 'No, no, *no*'.
Sign for 'drink': use same procedure as for 'food'.
Sign for 'hallo': say 'Hallo there, how are you?' or something of your choice, but keep to the same one.
Sign for 'play': say 'Shall we play?'—touch the baby's hand to his chest (you) then to yours (me) and then make the play sign.

WHY We must use speech as well as signs.

ACTION It may help you if you can see that your baby is communicating with you when he:

(a) asks for you to notice him, to share something he has noticed, to repeat something he has enjoyed, to alter something;

(b) smiles if you have met his needs, gets cross or cries when you have not met his needs;

(c) objects to something he does not like by pushing it away, struggling or crying hard;

(d) refuses to do something that is familiar more than once, to stop an activity he likes or pay attention to something by physically resisting or failing to do what you want;

(e) shows he has noticed the introduction or ending of something he likes or dislikes, or has noticed something different by perking up, changing his expression, touches or moves towards what he notices, changes his vocalisation, or begins to cry or laugh.

Try to respond to him so that he knows you are aware of what he is telling you—you may not be able to give him an answer, but at least respond in some way so that you are fostering the idea of communicating. It is so easy to do what the deaf/blind child indicates he wants or to ignore him (if you cannot do what he wants) without letting him know that his message has been received. If you can get a chance to hear a mother talking to a 1½- to 2½-year-old toddler, you will see how she acknowledges her child's communications before acting on them, and when he says 'ta' because he gets what he wants, she also acknowledges this response of his nine times out of ten by saying something like 'That's a good boy'. So much of this conversational method of communicating is lost to the deaf/blind child if we do not bear these things in mind.

LISTENING

Vibration

ACTION Whenever you want to draw your baby's attention to sound, make sure you use the 'alerting' word 'Listen' and make sure you have got his attention.

When you think he is noticing certain environmental sounds, like music on the radio, the hoover, or telephone, take him to what makes the sound and let him feel the vibrations. Encourage him to listen to and feel new sounds such as the engine of the car, the washing machine, Daddy's razor etc.

WHY We are not yet seeking to tell the baby what these things are or what they are for; we want to get him used to receiving information through his hands and to learn that different things vibrate in different ways. If he can connect the type of vibration with its source, this is fine—but we are still a long way off him connecting the fact that when his clothes are dirty it is necessary to put them in the big smooth box that goes thump-thump in order to get them clean again, but we are on the way.

68

Sounds he can make for himself

ACTION Show him how to make sounds with rattles, drums or squeakers with his hand on *yours*, then show him how to do it with your hands on his, making sure that one of his hands is on the noise maker to feel the vibration if this is possible. Remember to have the sound and then no sound for a few seconds so the child has a chance to change from listening *to* to listening *for*—if it is just a series of continuous noise, he will soon get bored. Do not use things that are similar—the more contrast there is between the sounds you want to interest him in, the more likely he is to be interested. When he does attempt to operate a sound maker himself, notice where he holds it—to one side more than the other, right against his ear?

WHY The child with useful hearing will get enjoyment from this kind of activity. By observing his responses we shall get quite a lot of information about what he hears and what he likes to hear and therefore the type of toys we should give him to play with when he is on his own.

Speech

ACTION Remember to talk to your child at his level, in front of him if he has some useful vision, close to his ear or his hearing aid. If you talk to him at some distance or above his level, he will be unlikely to hear. It is also important that he knows that it is a person speaking to him so that he gives his attention to the speaker. Every little clue we can give him helps—we should emphasise our facial expressions, gestures, body language as well as giving stress on the words we want him to learn to recognise. Although some of these things may be missed by a blind or severely partially sighted child, if we do remember, our communication style will be really lively and that in itself will be conveyed to the child.

WHY Speech has many components and each of us has our own characteristics of pitch, rhythm, intonation, speed of speaking and so on. We can also identify meaning by the length of sound, e.g. up=short sound, down=long sound. When we ask questions our voices rise at the end of a sentence, e.g. 'Want a sweet?'. When we make a statement in answer, our voices drop in intonation, e.g. 'Thanks very much'. When we give an instruction we maintain a level pitch, e.g. 'Stop that!'. Even if the deaf child cannot pick out some of the complex aspects of speech sounds, this kind of information may be of value to him.

ACTION Whenever possible when you are speaking to him, particularly when using the specific phrases, have your baby's hand on your face or throat.

WHY Because different sounds result from different lip shapes, and face vibrations, he will need these clues if he is to learn to speak, whether this is through partial hearing or by the Tadoma method.

69

Vocalising

ACTION Continue to note, and every so often take a short tape recording of, the sounds your baby makes. Whenever he makes nice vowel sounds, imitate them as you have done in the previous stage and encourage him in the turn-taking game: hands on your face and back on his own, or on his chest for his own vibrations. If he gets quite good at this, try changing the pitch. Make the contrast a very definite one—much higher and then much lower. Watch his reactions to this. Does he notice the difference? Does he try to change the sound he makes? Does he make no sound but try to change the shape of his mouth, even just the smallest mouth movement which would indicate he has an idea of what he has to do? Praise him for trying. When he can imitate this, make the difference less obvious or try a two-tone sound, e.g. a high 'aah' followed immediately by a low 'hah'—up/down to begin with, then down/up. Listen for any new sounds he might make and copy these. Remember the quiet gap between turn taking and give him time to practise on his own.

WHY These are all links in the long chain that has to be worked through slowly if a deaf child is to learn to speak—where there is the dual disability, even more slowly.

MOTOR DEVELOPMENT

ACTION Your baby should now be encouraged to roll from his tummy on to his back—again using a light or noise maker if necessary. Use the phrase 'Roll over' with nice intonation.

WHY The muscle development required to do this is essential to being able to stand and walk.

ACTION Encourage him to kick against a ball or balloon; when he is on his play rug, put it close to a settee or chair so that he can also kick and push against these.

ACTION When he is sitting on your lap, rock him from side to side, not giving him support (but having your hands close by in case of need) so that he has to do the work to keep him from losing his balance.

From lying to sitting

ACTION So long as there is now no head lag, encourage him to use some of the muscles he will need to use to get from lying to sitting by pulling gently on his arms when he is in the supine position and bringing him to the sitting position. Or you can raise his right shoulder, bringing his right hand towards the left so that he is leaning on his left shoulder; he then leans on his left elbow and finally his left hand, which brings him to the sitting position. Doing this in reverse will show him how to get back down again. (I suggest you try this out for yourself first!)

WHY By showing the baby what he will need to do while still not expecting him to do it for himself as yet, we are providing the experiences he would otherwise get visually.

ACTION Your baby should now sit alone briefly but will tend to fall sideways very easily (do not let this happen too often or he might be put off sitting). Show him how to put out his hand to save himself. Show him also, when he is sitting, how to lean forward slightly with his hands on the floor in front of him between his legs to help maintain his balance.

WHY Many deaf/blind children prefer to lie on their backs but they should be encouraged to sit as much as possible (still propped up most of the time) in order that their view of the world is more stimulating.

ACTION Sitting back on your knees with your baby in front of you and with his back to you, encourage him to support a little of his weight on his legs while being firmly held under his arms—you can play a little game of 'stand up, sit down' letting him come back to sit against your knees after a few seconds standing.

PLAY

ACTION Either on your lap or sitting with you on the floor in the 'hands-on' position, play the following games.

Sitting with you

1. Add another nursery rhyme with actions to the one you already use regularly—you might use 'Half a pound of tuppenny rice' because you can make a good climax.

2. Add to the sequence of movement pattern used in Stage 2, e.g. up/down, in/out, hands on lap/hands on head.

3. With palm upwards, touch each of your baby's fingers and his thumb in turn—do it to each hand—and sing little rhymes which you can make up yourself. (Finger awareness needs to be well developed for signing and finger spelling.)

Tactile information

4. With your hands over his, guide his hands over round things, e.g. balls of various sizes and textures (tennis, plastic, wool, foam; large ones, small ones). Give him the kind of whole-body movement that goes with the feeling of roundness. Use the special phrase 'round and round'.

Body awareness

5. Roll the balls down his arms and legs and over his body and head.

Tactile information

6. Have a number of little sealed bags filled with such things as dried beans, polystyrene bits, sand, buttons or similar things and help him to feel these (bags must all be made of the same material or they will distract from the differences in the contents). Alternatively, let him dabble his hands in little bowls containing this sort of material.

7. Half fill some small pill boxes (with safety lids) with the materials mentioned under (6), also having one with nothing at all in it, and encourage him to shake these and listen to the sounds they make.

8. Let him dabble his hands in a small bowl of warm water and then in one of cold water.

9. Put bracelets or rings on his arms and show him how to remove them, or a soft ball up his jumper and show him how to find it and remove it.

Rhythm

10. Have a tape recorder and a prepared tape which has on it 2 minutes of a happy tune with a good beat and then 2 minutes of a slow waltz-time rhythm. Put his hands on the recorder to let him feel the vibration, or with one hand on the recorder the other in yours, help him tap the recorder in time with the music.

Phrases for (8): 'It's hot, it's cold',

(9): '*Pull* it off', '*Pull* it out'.

With any of the above activities, do it only as long as the baby's interest holds—do not go on so long that it either upsets him or he experiences boredom. If any of the activities are really disliked, lay off them for a few days and then reintroduce them when he is in a happy mood. Choose one or two of the activities and use for a week or so regularly, then try some of the others. They all contain many learning experiences which will be of value as time goes on.

Signal

ACTION When you want to pick your baby up from the sitting position, use the same signal as for picking up from lying down—tap his arms gently.

Play sitting in a chair

ACTION If you have a small rocking chair with a front bar to it or a baby swing with bars all round, your baby could have short periods in these now.

ACTION A chair with a tray in front—preferably with a non-slip surface and a rim round the edge to stop toys rolling off—is good both for play alone and with you. If you can make several trays to fit over the top of the natural tray, this could help the baby anticipate the activity, e.g. a vinyl-covered one for meals, one with a black surface so that the toys show up (particularly yellow ones), or a transparent plastic one in place of the original through which you could shine a torch on the toys you wished him to search for and play with. If the tray goes well round the child, he is encouraged to reach further and to move more to get the toys. Choose toys that are bright, have a nice shape, different surface textures, some that make a noise and some that he can bang with—when he has a new one, watch his reactions and the way he handles it, then show him what he can do with it and how to explore it. Expect him to want to mouth things a great deal now and encourage this as long as it is for information and is not becoming an obsessive habit, e.g. he does nothing with things except mouth them.

ACTION Encourage him to transfer things from one hand to the other and to hold two things, one in each hand, at the same time, if he is not already doing this.

WHY To grasp and feel are skills necessary for gathering tactile information, the right hand to grasp, the left hand to explore (or vice versa if the child has a dominant left hand). Mouthing is a source of information for all children and some deaf/blind children use their lips as a checkpoint all their lives for some things.

72

Sitting on the floor

ACTION When he is sitting on the floor, still well propped up if alone, put things where his hands or feet will knock up against them, or put things in the space between his legs, or hang things on a rail in front of him so that he can reach forward and find them. If some of the toys are on thin elastic, they will bounce back when he lets go of them. If he picks something up and drops it, take his hand in the direction which the toy has fallen and show him how to search round for it, and be very excited when you both find it again (even though you may have had to move it to where he could find it). If he has enough vision, make him look at where you find it, using a torch beam to encourage the searching and finding if this helps.

WHY All part and parcel of learning that, even when we cannot see things or people, they still exist—provides stability. It would be very confusing if we were never certain whether we should find all our household things there each morning—vision confirms this for us and we soon take it for granted that they will be there and so will everything else unless we or some other persons change it. There is a delay of about 6 months in the blind child acquiring the concept of object permanence—it may be longer where there is the dual disability.

Playing on the floor

On tummy

ACTION You can now make his floor rug more interesting by sewing on to it such things as plastic rings, large buttons, pieces of fur, silk etc., for him to discover with his hands or his feet. Put some toys his arm's length away and shine a torch on them so that he is encouraged to stretch to reach them, or attract his attention to a toy by the noise it makes or by banging it on the floor for him to feel the vibration.

WHY We have to make life interesting in the way that it interests him: he must find familiar experiences and new ones, and when the new ones have themselves become familiar, he needs more new ones.

On his back

Body awareness

ACTION Make four or five little bags, about 6 inches square, and fill these with sand; seal them well. Put one of these on his chest and show him how to find it and take it off with both hands. Then put it on the left side and show him how to move it off with his left hand and similarly with the right hand. When he can do this, you can put a little bag on his foot or another part of his body and get him to find and move it—and, if he enjoys this game, you can work up to putting several little bags on different parts. You can also put the bags under parts of his body where it is possible for him to reach them.

ACTION He will need to have some time sitting and some lying, but as his back becomes stronger and he sits without falling because his balance is improving, increase the sitting time and decrease the time he plays on his back.

ACTION He can also play over a roll or foam wedge, but you need to put some sort of barrier to confine the toys to the space within which he can reach.

Visual training

ACTION Spend a few minutes every day doing the following little exercises—make a game of it for him, knowing yourself that however little vision he has, if he is to be able to use it most efficiently, he needs the skills these exercises promote.

1. You need two people, one holding baby on her lap with his back to her and the other holding a bright toy or toy with a torch beam lighting it up. (To prevent the child looking at the torch rather than the toy, put a long black sleeve on the torch.) Hold the

Visual tracking

toy in the position and at the distance you know the baby is most likely to spot it. When he has seen it, move it from the midline:

 (a) to one side,

 (b) to the other side,

 (c) upwards,

 (d) downwards.

Observe how far it has to go in either of the directions before he loses it.

You can also do this exercise using a bright torch moving behind a sheet of coloured plastic material, preferably transparent.

When using a toy, after tracking it without being allowed to reach for it, if he reaches out for it, let him have it.

2. Play give-and-take games—Mummy holding baby shows him how to grasp the toy Daddy is offering him, then how to offer it back to Daddy—have lots of fun over this game.

3. Play a hiding game—Daddy puts tissue over his face, Mummy shows the baby it is there and helps him pull it off; 'peep-bo' says Daddy (whose face needs to be quite near the baby's). The tissue can then be put over the baby's face and over Mummy's with the same pantomime. You can use lots of nice phrases in this (and the above games) such as '*Give* it to Daddy', 'Look, look'—the sort of action words which will be amongst the signs your baby will be needing to learn soon.

WHY Games like this, as well as providing visual stimulation for the baby, also stress turn taking which is so basic to both communicating and socialising.

ACTION Either with a torch beam on a dark wall or using a torch beam on a toy, light up a spot (or toy) and when the child has spotted it, turn off the light for a few seconds, then light up again in a different place, but not very far away from the original place, and see if baby can relocate it. (If using a toy, have the room darkened and do not let him see you move it.)

WHY This helps the child to learn to move quickly from one fixation to another.

74

Focusing

ACTION Begin to encourage your baby to learn to focus in the following ways.

1. Have a line of shiny things going away from him and shine a torch on each in turn, going further away each time.
2. With Mummy holding the baby over her shoulder and Daddy behind her, Mummy moves away; Daddy moves towards them, keeping himself in the line of the child's vision—a sort of 'chase me' game.

ACTION Remember, *seeing* when you have poor vision requires a lot of concentration which the baby may not possess yet. It is also very tiring to have to concentrate, so there should be short periods of these games with other kinds of play in between.

ACTION Deaf/blind children often have a habit of throwing toys—generally to the back of them. It is part of the seeing/hearing child's natural play because it is fun to crawl to find them again. It may be for the fun of it or to get rid of things (although he does it with the toys he likes as well as those he does not like), but he ends up with nothing to play with—when it also applies to the mug with his milk or the dish with his food, it is not such fun for Mummy. If you can catch his hand just before he throws a toy, if he has developed this habit, and show him how to put it down (using the phrase 'Put it *down*') so that it is there for him to reach and get again, it does help. As far as the mug is concerned, one mother had solved the problem of throwing by having a heavy mug which it was impossible for her little girl to throw—it had to be put down!

ACTION In all your baby's play activities, watch how he handles toys: how does he use his hands to hold them, for there is a natural sequence for this (see Appendix No. 1)? Is he reaching for things more accurately? How much time does he spend exploring something new? Can you spot the features by which he recognises something familiar? Does he have a favourite toy? Do you think he notices different colours? If we can answer some of these questions, we shall find he is telling us a lot about his abilities and the way he learns—and this in turn gives us clues as to what we need to provide to help him make further progress.

Romping

ACTION Deaf/blind children love movement—being swung round and round, held high and brought down quickly, held upside down and so on. They like being on swings and being swung on a blanket between two people. These provide opportunities for nice phrases like '*Up* you go, *down* you come' and for the child to make some body sign for the activity to continue (or you can give him a hand signal related to the activity—hand waving round and round as a signal for being whirled round and round in your arms).

By himself in pram

ACTION Continue to have bright mobiles etc. where he can watch them, and move these to different positions so that sometimes he has to move himself to see them.

ROUTINES

Feeding

ACTION Encourage him to mouth rusks, dry toast—plain or with a touch of Marmite. Continue to increase the variety and texture of the solids, thickening them up very gradually. Keep the flavours separate. If he seems to dislike something the first time he tastes it, this may be because it is unfamiliar. Unless you find it puts him off the whole meal, give him just one spoonful of the new food before he has something familiar—if it is because it is new, once he is used to the one spoonful and accepts this without a fuss, give him more of it. He should be sitting well enough to sit in a high chair, and he should have a little spoon of his own to hold during the feed. He must be well established on solids before we begin to show him how to feed himself. If he mouths the spoon, put just a tiny taste of his food on it—paving the way.

WHY Being too long on thin foods tends to encourage constipation which can become a major problem later on. It is also easy for these children, who miss the enticement of seeing the food, to get hooked on to one texture or flavour and refuse to take anything else—sometimes throughout all the preschool years. This is more likely to occur if weaning is delayed beyond the normal time and often there are good reasons why this is so. A good, varied diet is necessary for good health.

Using a cup

ACTION Start using a cup now (with or without a special top), just for a mouthful or two in place of the spoonfuls he has been having from Stage 2. He is more likely to take this at a time when he is really thirsty. Sucking needs to be phased out to prepare for chewing.

ACTION Remember food and drink have become separate items now. Use the appropriate signs. With the food, you can now, after signing 'food', let the baby smell it, feel the bowl and feel the food that is in it with his fingers. Also remember to do this from behind him ('hands on'). Encourage him to smell the food on his fingers and to put them to his mouth. Sign 'food' again and put in the first spoonful—if, when you are feeding him (from behind), you can get him to rest his hand on yours as you lift up the spoon and then put it back to the bowl to refill it, this will give him some preliminary information about what he will have to do to feed himself when the time comes.

Bathing

ACTION When he is being washed, show the baby how to hold the sponge or small flannel and rub it over his tummy. Show him how to splash with both his hands and his feet. Encourage him to be on his tummy in the bath (not very much water). Let him smell the soap and feel it when it is dry and when it is wet. Let him help you shake the talc on to his tum and rub it in. Any way in which he can be, involve him in the bathing routine. It is never too soon to involve a deaf/blind baby in something that actually impinges on his own body, and what better time than bathing. It needs to be an unhurried and enjoyable experience for you both; it is full of learning opportunities, and lots of nice special phrases: '*Shake* the powder', '*Splash* the water' etc.

Body image

ACTION After bathing, continue to work to the massage programme and play all sorts of games that help the child to become aware of his body—help him to rub himself or pat himself, find his toes and so on.

Dressing and undressing

ACTION Keep to the same sequences as previously.
Watch to see if your baby now is beginning to anticipate this—puts his arms out when it is time for sleeves before you have actually given him the signal that this is to happen, or holds out his leg for the sock to come off after you have taken off his shoe.

When you are undressing him, show him how to pull off the last bit of his socks (get them off as far as the toes so he can do the rest). Encourage him to take something off over his head after you have got it almost off.

When you have been out and come back home, show him how to pull off his hat—if he does this when you are out, you have a lovely opportunity to use the word/sign 'No'!

Remember that dressing and undressing should be done in the 'hands-on' position so that his body is correctly positioned and you can make him aware of the feeling of pushing forward to get his arms and legs into his clothes.

Toiletting

ACTION Preparation only—Stage 2.
Now try sitting him on the potty without the nappy over it, still between your knees (you can be sitting or kneeling) so that he is close to you. Do this for a few minutes *every* time his nappy is changed during the *day*.

ENVIRONMENTAL

ACTION Take him with you when you go to make the beds. First take him to his own cot and let him hold his own pillow and show him how to punch it up. Then go to your own room, let him feel the pillows on which you have placed/pinned/fixed the tactile clues which you use for yourself and Daddy (a hankie with your scent on or your brooch, Daddy's tiepin or lapel badge—whichever he uses to recognise you both) and let him feel these. Let him also feel you making the 'sleep' sign—do your best to let him make the connection, the use of your bed for you and his bed, that you go to sleep just as he does.

In time, you can extend this to other bedrooms, using their occupants' tactile clues to identify them. If it is possible, also have these on the doors of the room in some way so that as you go into the room, letting him help you push the door open, he also begins to know that there are different rooms and these are used by different people. All these things a seeing baby would learn through vision, a blind child by being made to feel them and being told about them—it may seem a tedious task with the deaf/blind child, but how else is he to know these things exist?

Stairs

ACTION Stairs. I am sure you have been giving him the feeling of movement associated with going up and down the stairs and have been saying 'up, up, up and down, down, down'. Now sit with him on the stairs sometimes and encourage him to feel them and the way they go higher or lower. (A word of warning—do not use a phrase like '*up* to bed', we go upstairs for lots of reasons and if the child associates going upstairs only with going to bed, he may not want to go at other times.) It would be best to begin using the phrase 'Up, up the stairs and down, down the stairs' so that when the time comes for the sign 'stairs' we have a link.

Kitchen

ACTION In the kitchen, decide on a strong but pleasant smell which he is always given the opportunity to experience whenever he goes into the kitchen with you. When you have him beside you as you are cooking the meals, let him smell, touch, and even taste some foods before they are cooked and after they are cooked—he will not make the connections yet, but you are preparing him for the time when his experiences allow him to realise that food is cooked and how it changes in all these aspects. If you are using a blender or beater, let him feel the vibrations. When you are washing up, let him feel those 'nice soft bubbles' that are so good for your hands, or have a little bowl of his own. What sort of things in a kitchen would a seeing/hearing child want to hold and play with—wooden spoon, custard powder lids, saucepan lids, scourers? Why not the deaf/blind baby? So long as these things happen only in this place, the kitchen, they are all clues that help him to recognise the difference between that and other rooms.

ACTION Before you take him outdoors—for a walk or ride in the car—take him to the front door, put his hand over yours as you open it, step outside and let him be aware briefly of the change in the temperature and amount of light. Go back in and dress him, then take your walk.

WHY Of course, your baby will not absorb all this information at once, but if it occurs regularly enough, bits of it will be remembered gradually and begin to be linked together, eventually making a whole. He has to know all about a thing before he can *use* a sign for it—we are making him aware of these things. He is still too young to know what they are for and how we use them—the wooden spoon is a nice thing to feel and to bang with, no more than that, but at least he knows it exists. Giving your baby these experiences is a time-consuming operation, yet without this help his knowledge of his world would be very poor. This is why you must seek help and allow your baby to spend some time with people other than yourself.

Stage 4

INTRODUCTION

So far your baby has been taken to things or they have been taken to within his grasp. Now, in this stage, comes the beginning of the greatest step forward of all—that of learning how to move himself from place to place and that by doing this he can find for himself not only those things which are already familiar to him, but lots and lots more exciting things. With luck we have whetted his appetite and provided enough motivation for him to want to move beyond the 'sitting circle' which up to now has been the extent of his exploration. Of course we will be beside him still to guide and help him, but we want the motivation to come from within him. We want to provide him with the information *he* seeks, not always that which *we* think he should have—although sometimes we shall engineer the situation so that it encourages him to seek useful information.

We hope that we will see signs that he is learning to anticipate some of the regular routines, accepts our guidance 'hands on' and the manipulation of his hands to make the signs which we have introduced, and that he enjoys the play periods. In Stage 4 we shall move forward in all these areas, building on what he has learned already. Remember, children do not always develop at the same rate in each area. Sometimes they leap ahead in one and, while they are coping with the new skills in this, will regress in others temporarily. The deaf/blind child has a less efficient way of remembering, so will need reminding more often and for a longer time. If the new items seem to need to be broken down into smaller steps, you should now be able to do this for yourself. Look at the goal, the various things involved in getting there—movement patterns, the environment and necessary objects together with the level the child is at—write them down and I am sure you will know what to do. It is much more pleasant to have found a way for yourself and to take full credit for having helped your child to achieve the aim.

Although we would not expect your baby to be using signs even in imitation yet, look out for any little movement in context which might suggest he is at the stage the seeing/hearing baby is, when he might make the sound 'mmmmm' as the first stage towards saying 'Mummy'. The seeing/hearing child has to hear the word 'Mummy' many hundreds of times before he is able to use it with meaning; from having just a few words, he quickly acquires a great many. So it will be with the deaf/blind child—once he begins to use a few signs, signing can become a real tool for communicating. He has to be shown many times before he can execute the right movement, he has to have it many many times in context before he can make an association between the sign and what it stands for—only after this can the two aspects merge so that *he* is able to make the sign with meaning. We are laying the foundations for this during the early stages.

Perhaps this is where I should explain the reason for the choice of words/signs and phrases to be used in the programme, and why it is necessary to stick to these (or any that you might decide to substitute). First and foremost, the word/sign must refer to the actual thing or event we want the child to link it to: take the word 'toilet', which we also call lavatory, loo, bathroom and use interchangeably, but which would be too complex for the deaf/blind child. We use toilet because this is the word most likely to be used in school and in places outside the home. It is also often better at this early stage of communication to use a word that is related to an action or state rather than the object being used. For instance '*Dry* yourself' after bathing rather than 'Here's the towel': the effect on the child is to become dry, he can learn 'towel' later and he will find them in many places other than the bathroom and for uses other than getting dry after a bath. For the deaf/blind child 'cup' must stand for the thing from which he drinks—it will be quite a time before we can draw his attention to the differences in drinking things as a reason for them being called mugs, glasses, tumblers, tankards and so on.

Lastly, the 'hands-on' technique now becomes very important as the child's ability to use his hands develops and he increasingly uses these for information about things and what to do with them. To accept this way of learning from us, the closeness at which we must be together in order that the tactile and kinaesthetic information can pass between us, the relationship between us has to be good and he must trust us—at the same time we must recognise any attempts at being independent and doing something himself and give him this freedom.

The Programme: Stage 4

RELATIONSHIP

ACTION With a growing awareness of other people comes a growing awareness of himself as a person and, if we have been successful in encouraging the idea of communicating, the baby may be beginning to realise how he can influence people by crying, by doing or by not doing certain things. 'I am' leads to 'I want' and 'I cannot wait', and because it is so difficult to get over to him the reason why he cannot have or may have to wait, he often becomes very frustrated and sometimes this boils over into a temper tantrum. It is equally frustrating to us not to be able to reason with the baby. There are two ways of dealing with this kind of situation: observe the occasions when the problem arises and alter these so that they do not occur in the first place, or provide a distraction before boiling point is reached. Remember, it is not the baby's fault that he cannot yet understand and if he does get upset he will want a lot of loving to reassure him. He must always know that although we may not always like what he *does*, we always love *him*.

COMMUNICATION

ACTION With the awareness that he can influence what happens to him, he is ready to begin to be shown that the movements we have been making with his hands to indicate what is going to happen can also be used by him for the same purpose. The sign for 'please' is a good one to begin with—in much the same way as we encourage the seeing/hearing baby to say 'ta'.

New signs

The sign is made by clasping the hands together, fingers over the side of each hand. If it is easier, you can initially just hold the two palms together.

Begin using this sign when he is playing a game with two people passing things backwards and forwards—when one passes him the toy, before the other person helps him or lets him take it, she just briefly brings his hands together to say 'please', meaning in effect 'Please may I have it' (later on the same sign is used to say 'thank you'). You can then extend it to situations in which the child reaches out for something and you help him make this sign before he is allowed to have it. It may have to be used many times before he catches on, but we have actually been surprised how quickly young deaf/blind children do learn to use it themselves to ask for something.

You can also begin to use it in conjunction with food and drink. *Procedure.* You sign 'You (want) drink', asking the question with good intonation and letting the child know the drink is there by briefly touching the cup. You then help him make the sign for 'please' before having it. Touching the cup should link the sign for

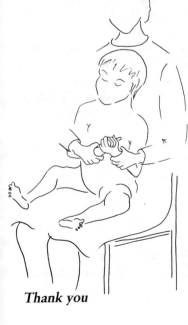

Thank you

81

drink with the drink and the 'please' sign as a means of getting it. *Sign No. 2* is that for 'wait', for the reasons given under 'Relationship'.

Here we use the same sign as for 'please' but put the clasped hands down on to the child's lap with a little push, saying firmly 'wait'. It will not be an easy one for him to understand, but try to find situations in which it can become meaningful, e.g. while you are winding up a toy for him. If it can be used when the pressure to hurry is not too great to start with, it will be more likely to be effective later on when the child is, say, hungry and the meal is not ready.

Signs No. 3 and 4 are those for going out.

Walking: make a walking movement with your index and second finger down the child's wrist and on to the palm. Show him how to do this on himself and on you.

In the car: take the child's hands and turn an imaginary steering wheel.

Use these just before you are going out and again when you actually go out—the 'car' one also again as you put the baby into his car seat.

Sign No. 5 is one that says 'finished', 'no more', 'all gone'.

You hold the baby's one hand in the form of a fist and tap it sharply on to the palm of the other twice.

This is not the orthodox sign, but one which we have found is easily recognised by deaf/blind children. By using the quick double tap, we feel it should not be confused with the similar single tap which represents 'G' in the Finger Spelling method (which your child might use when he goes to school). This sign, like 'please', is one that can be used very frequently. Used at the end of a game in the first place to indicate 'We have finished but are going to do something else just as nice', it can be emphasised by letting the baby be aware that you are putting away the toys you have been playing with, or by changing the position in which you play. As this meaning is recognised it can also have meaning in a situation where there literally is no more of something the baby wants very badly. Once you have said 'all gone' in this way, stick to it, or it will have no meaning for the child at all.

The correct sign for 'bedtime' is putting both hands to one side of the head—this was too difficult for the small baby to do, but should present no problems now.

ACTION Watch baby's actions with objects: is he beginning to imitate some of the things you have been doing with him, e.g. taking his hands round a ball as if recognising its shape? Is he beginning to expect that you do something with things and, if so, when he cannot do it for himself or does not know what to do, does he put his hand on yours to indicate that he wants your help? If so, we have reached a recognised stage in the development of communication in all children. He is consciously making an approach to you to help him or share with him some activity,

82

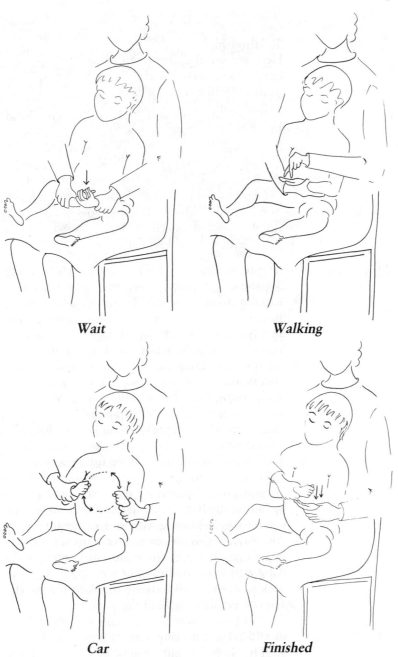

Wait   *Walking*

Car   *Finished*

knowing what he wants and knowing you are the one who can respond. People and things and their relationship to him are beginning to be sorted out. In our play and our routines we must now provide him with the opportunity to make this kind of approach to us so that communication, in addition to being useful, can grow to being purposeful.

VOCALISING   ACTION Continue to play at reciprocal sound making, always giving the tactile and vibration clues through your face and

83

throat. If he can now imitate some of the two-tone sounds, encourage him to make the same sound several times, e.g. ba-ba-ba-ba-ba and ma-ma-ma-ma. Give him different vowel sounds, making him aware of the way the shape of the mouth changes, e.g. between saying 'eeee' and 'ahahah'. He may like to hear these sounds best when you make them close to his ear and will probably show you this by pulling your head towards him for more. If any of the sounds he makes seem to be something like any of the words you emphasise in your special phrases and are in context, show him you have recognised these by giving him back the normal word and praising him for his effort.

Continue to record short snatches of his sound making. The blind child with no hearing loss shows some delay in the development of speech and language, so we must expect this even more with a deaf/blind child.

LISTENING

ACTION Being guided by your baby's responses to the listening experiences you have been giving him, introduce more sound-making toys, particularly those which he can operate for himself—squeaky things, a hooter with a rubber squeeze bulb (good for sound and hand skills). If you use a sound maker, is he beginning to turn to locate it? If not, put his hand to the position where you sounded it. Chime bars are quite fun to use together—one at each end of the scale to provide contrast. Listening means that you take notice of the sounds you hear; the next step is to notice the difference between the sounds you hear and to be able to say 'This sound goes with this thing, that sound goes with that thing', so it is most important that your baby, when he shows he has heard something, is then given the opportunity to feel and explore that thing or he will not be able to make the connection. At this stage, although your baby might be able to hear the sound of a train (real or on tape), it could not represent a train—he could show you that he recognised the sound but not know what made it. We now want to help him learn what it is that makes the sound he recognises and, where possible, what has to be done to that thing in order that it makes a sound, e.g. push a button to put on the radio, bang the drum. So choose carefully the sounds you offer him.

MOTOR DEVELOPMENT

ACTION Once your baby is sitting, well balanced, encourage him not only to reach things, but also to turn to the side (either side) to take something from you.

WHY Helps to achieve balance while rotating the spine.

ACTION Encourage him to slide forward on his bottom (by pushing on one leg and one hand) to reach a toy.

WHY Some children do not crawl, so need another way to get around. It is better to go both ways, but they must have one way at least if they are to be able to explore.

84

ACTION Encourage him to creep, that is, to crawl with his tummy on the floor. In this position, show him how to bring each leg up under his body while pressing the other against something hard.

WHY Preparation for real crawling so long as all four limbs are involved, as it helps the spine to become more flexible.

ACTION With knees tucked under his body, show him how to support himself on his outstretched hands and then bring him back to sit on his knees with his arms still supporting him. Rock him gently from side to side in this position to increase his ability to balance and to strengthen his back muscles.

ACTION With his tummy off the floor, show him how to move one arm forward and then the other; follow this up with moving one leg forward and then the other. These single movements need to be practised a great many times before the child will be ready to learn to crawl properly (which requires that the child moves the left arm and right knee, then the right arm and left knee).

WHY Although some children do miss out on crawling, it is quite important that we should provide the experiences which enable the deaf/blind child to crawl, for in addition to giving him a means to explore sooner than if we wait for him to learn to walk, it also helps to strengthen the head and upper limb control which is often delayed in the child with a visual disability.

Crawling ACTION The help of two people is required for showing him how to learn to crawl cross-laterally (moving opposite arms and legs simultaneously). One manipulates the legs, the other the arms—working up to the child being able to move his arms forward for himself, then his legs by himself, and finally managing to do both on his own. Always reward him for effort and keep these and the exercises above which work towards this skill quite short, but used regularly several times a day.

WHY Crawling exercises the child's hands and the cross-lateral use of limbs is a preparation for walking which requires the same procedure.

ACTION When the baby is crawling well, encourage him to reach forwards and sideways for an object to help to increase his balance.

ACTION When he is lying on his tummy and on his back, help him to stretch out his legs and arms. If you can obtain a large beach ball or physiotherapy ball (recommended diameter equal to or greater than the height of the child), lie him across this and, rocking him back and forth, show him how it feels to have his feet on the floor one side and then his hands on the floor over the other side.

Pre-standing WHY This helps to get him used to the feeling of being upright and is preparation for standing alone and then walking.

ACTION Sit on the floor and encourage him to stand facing you with his feet flat on the floor, taking some of his weight if not all. Gently move his arms up and down and encourage him to bend his knees when his hands are down. He may make some stepping movements—show great pleasure at all his efforts.

PLAY

ACTION All the above motor developmental exercises must be done as play. Whenever possible, join in with him—crawl with him, over and beside him, roll towards him and away from him and get him to imitate you, sit and rock with him from side to side—he gains information from your body as to how to move his own.

ACTION The following new games can now be introduced.

On your lap

1. Play a game of shaking baby's hands, arms, legs and head, making up a little rhyme stressing the names of the body parts.
2. Stick bits of shiny, coloured Christmas Sellotape on parts of his body and help him to find them and pull them off.

Body awareness

3. Shine a light on various parts of his body and get him to touch the light spot.
4. With as much of your body as possible in contact with his, take your baby's hands and move them: (a) up and down in sweeping movements, and (b) in circles. Make these movements as big as the child's arms allow and do them very rhythmically.

Imitation

When you have done either of these a few times, stop just before completing the movement and see if the child's own movements suggest he would know how to continue and complete it.
5. Play any of the well-known action games which encourage baby to touch his head, eyes, nose, mouth and ears—let him feel yours and play the game again touching you.
6. Play finger games or action songs which require a pattern of movement like 'The wheels of the bus'.
7. You rub his arm (leg, hand or face) then, 'hands on', show him how to do the same on you.

ACTION Games with music.
Make a music tape which is blank for a minute or so after each 2 minutes of music. With the baby on your lap and his feet on the tape recorder (if he likes this), show him how to clap when he can hear/feel the music is playing and to stop when it stops.

Play

If you can play a guitar, let your baby have his hands on the instrument when you play, or gently strum his fingers across while you finger the chords. You can also show him how to press down the stops on an autoharp while you pluck the strings.

WHY Music by itself at this age quickly becomes boring—it is being able to do something to or to make music that creates interest in it.

Object permanence

ACTION Show him how to hide a toy under a cushion, tissue or small box and then how to find it again—this is an opportunity for having fun and for making him feel, through your behaviour, that it is exciting.

86

WHY If he can play this game, we can be pretty sure he has got the idea of object permanence. To find hidden things is a useful skill later on in specific learning situations, e.g. colour matching.

Action toys

ACTION Introduce more toys that 'do' things, for instance a toy helicopter on which the rotor blade revolves, a wind-up merry-go-round, a sparkler toy, a vibrating toothbrush holder on which you can put lots of different tops—almost any small toy that requires a simple action to activate it. To begin with, you let the child have your hand under his when you operate the switch or key, then let him feel the result of what you have done. When it runs down and he wants more, you have an ideal situation in which to see if he takes your hand and puts it to the toy for you to operate it, *and* before you do it to get him to sign 'please'. The next stage is for you to take his hand and show him what he must do to operate the toy (he will have had some preparation for this from the movement he felt when his hand was on yours). When he can learn to operate it himself, what a boost for you both. If he really delights in toys of this kind, you can give him some signals for him to use to choose which of two toys he would like, e.g. index finger pointing up and going round in a circle for the helicopter, or make a whirring noise with his hand on your throat for the vibrating toy. This is quite an advanced stage, so do not be disappointed if it is quite some time before he can make a choice; but giving him the opportunity prepares for that time.

WHY By communicating he is learning that he can influence people. Now, in play, he is learning that he can also influence objects. 'I do' leads to 'What else can I do?'—encompassing in time 'What can I do for myself?' and 'for other people?'.

ACTION Introduce one or two toys that can be pulled by a string and show him how, by pulling the string, he can get the toys he cannot as yet go and get for himself, for example small plastic lorries and cars or animals on wheels because when he does handle them, the wheels are fun to feel spinning round and learn to spin for himself.

WHY Hands are tools, but there are also other things besides hands which are tools (e.g. the spoon to eat with).

ACTION Now he is able to play sitting, have a few toys in a box (or there is a plastic picnic basket with a two-sided top which is ideal for this activity), and show him how to find them one at a time, examine them or play with them. If you have two boxes, he can take them out of one and put them into the other (fix these together with a clip so they remain together).

ACTION The following games will encourage the child with some useful vision to improve its use. For the child with very little vision, the objects need to be lit up or to be painted with fluorescent paint and used in a dark room. For the blind child with some hearing, these exercises can be used with sound makers and sound location. You need two people.

Ocular co-ordination

Visual training

1. Hold two toys in front of baby, one at the midline, the other 6″ to 12″ to the side, and encourage him to reach out and touch one and then the other, using the right hand when the object is to the right, the left hand when it is to the left. Work one side then the other, not across. You can change the position of the outer object so that baby can be encouraged to look up and down. You could also use a squeaky toy which he has to reach out and squeeze, or something he could bang.

2. Hold objects so that in order to move from one to the other he must look from one side to the other, crossing the midline—make the distance between them quite small to begin with. Encourage him to touch the one to the right with his right hand, the one to the left with his left hand; then let him hold both hands together and touch the two objects, one at a time.

3. Hold a large object for which the child needs to use two hands (big ball, balloon) within easy reach and get him to reach out and grasp it. If he tends not to look at it, but reaches without looking, move it a little away so that he has to look for it to get it.

ACTION Whenever an opportunity to make your child look for something occurs, take advantage of it. Do not always give a toy you are playing with directly to him; let him see it and move it away a bit so that he has to track its course in order to reach to the right place for it. If, for instance, you were showing him how to put rings on a stick and getting him to take them from you before putting them on together, offer him one from the right, one from the left and so on—make him use his vision as much as you can in this way. If he is to use his vision, he must practise looking.

The following are more ideas to encourage tracking.

1. Fix bright, shiny paper on cardboard shapes and stick these on to ice-cream sticks. Sit with your child on your lap at one side of a small table and get someone to move the sticks so that the shapes move along the edge of the table.

2. Get a 2-ft piece of dowling with a string on one end to which you can tie various bright things. Dangle these in front of him one at a time and get him to follow as you move them, left to right, right to left, up and down, and if baby manages to follow these, then see if he can follow them diagonally.

3. Blow soap bubbles and see if your baby can follow them and reach out and pop them.

Play by himself

ACTION Discourage him from lying on his back unless it is part of the motor development games, but encourage him to lie on his tummy, putting more interesting things on and *under* his play rug that will entice him to try to creep to get them.

ACTION Just sitting can become boring, so give him lots of different sitting experiences—in a rubber tyre, on a beanbag, on a small rocking horse, a clothes basket, small child's chair. A cardboard box is another nice play place—toys in it cannot roll away, they can be hung on the sides and, if another half-box is put upside down in the big box, there you have a table.

ACTION Do not give your baby a pile of allsorts to play with; give him different selections of toys that have something in common, e.g. a set of things for shape, or colour (the same), or sound, or texture—talk to him about them and show him how to explore and look at them before leaving him to play as he wishes with them. You can also give him a set of things that are connected with daily routines—a cup, a spoon, hairbrush, sponge etc.—to explore and play with. (Watch to see if he knows how to use any of these: does the spoon go to his mouth, the brush to his hair? If not, remind him of their use before he plays with them.) Make a new set of noise-making cartons (all covered in the same bright material) which include some that do not make any noise at all, and encourage him to shake these; make a similar set (different covering) which have different quantities of sand in them (some with none) and watch to see how he handles these (for weight).

A toy he might like and which encourages him to notice different textures (suggested by an Australian teacher) is made by joining lots of different pieces of nice-textured materials and putting this into a container, in the lid of which there is a hole for the child to pull the material through. You could make several different strips.

ROUTINES

Feeding

ACTION Because we have been giving your baby lots of things to hold, encouraging him to use his hands, it is to be hoped that he has not minded holding such things as toast or hard biscuits and that now he is beginning to put them to his mouth and, with some teeth through, is starting to chew them. Marmite and honey seem to be favourite things to put on to these dry foods. The consistency of his food should certainly now be mashed rather than being put through the Mouli mixer. He should begin to have less help with holding his cup and perhaps manage by himself if he can have a cup with two handles. There may be some spilling as he has to learn to cup his lip to prevent this.

Stage 1 of feeding himself should be begun. Standing behind the baby (who is in his high chair), sitting behind him if he is in a low chair, put the spoon in his dominant hand and, holding his other hand on the dish, show him how to put the spoon in the dish, scoop some food on it and bring it to his mouth—pause before putting it to his lips to give him time to open his mouth. Begin this routine with something you know he really likes, and if he resists, just make him do it for the first mouthful every day at one mealtime until he gets used to the idea, then two mouthfuls, increasing slowly until he, with your help, is holding the spoon for the whole dishful.

WHY Feeding has alway been something very much associated with mother, and for the deaf/blind child this is a habit he seems reluctant to break. However, it is usually a child's first self-help skill so, once started, we should persist until familiarity breaks down the resistance.

Bathing

ACTION Let the baby feel the bath with no water in it, feel the tap being turned and the water coming from it (not too hot) and then feel the water in the bath. At the end of bathing, pull out the plug (*you* do this because if you show him how to do it, you may have an empty bath sooner than you want); then help him become aware that all the water is gone and, when it has all gone, give him the 'all gone' sign, and lift him out right away. When he is in the bath, show him how to rub more parts of his body with the sponge and also let him wash your hand and arm. When he is out, show him how to do a little bit of the drying. Use the phrases '*Wash* your arm', '*Dry* your tummy'. Let him have some toys in the bath—some that wind up and swim along for him to follow visually, some that you can pour water through for him to watch—a plastic washing-up liquid container pushed under the water makes a lovely noise and air bubbles you can feel. These days there are also some toys which you can hang on the side of the bath and which, if the water is poured into them, are activated in some way. Your baby can feel all things if he cannot manage to see them. Water is generally a joy to deaf/blind children and they become good swimmers later on.

Dressing and undressing

ACTION Now that your baby is sitting well, it is preferable if you can both undress and dress him while you sit on the floor with him between your legs and your hands in the 'hands on' position. With prompting, he should now be able to do some more of the taking off by himself—pulling off his shoe and his sock once it is over the heel, his pants once they are down to his ankles, taking his arms out of sleeves (so long as you hang on to the sleeve) and pulling things over his head.

When dressing, he should be encouraged to pull up the last bit of his socks, to put his arm into the sleeve held out for him and wriggle his hand through the end, and he should be able to pull on things just put over the top of his head.

If he can do these things, he is telling you that he recognises the routine, can anticipate what to do next and can even do a bit for himself. If he cannot do them yet, do not worry but keep encouraging by prompting and by giving him lots of praise when he makes a good try.

Toiletting

Stage 3. The potty should now be on the floor and he should be sat on it for a minute or so at *every* nappy change. In Appendix 5 you will find a toiletting chart which I would suggest you might now begin to use as preparation for toilet training proper. You make a copy of this and fill it in for a couple of weeks and then look at it to see if there are any regular times when your baby is either wet or has a dirty nappy. If there is a regular time, begin to put him on the potty 5 or 10 minutes before the time this happens, and see if you get any results. You may have to keep at this for a month or two and it may seem very tedious, but because it is so difficult to get over to a child who has the dual handicap exactly what we want of him, it does take longer for him to become toilet trained—this way does make the chances of catching him more likely.

In the summer months when you can let him be free of nappies and in trainer pants (or at other times if you can put up with a few accidents), you are more likely to get him to understand what you want. Never scold him for an accident; let him feel the wet and then touch the potty, at the same time reminding him of the sign for toilet, rubbing his hips as if taking off his pants. If he likes sweets, I personally would reward him this way when he does begin using his potty so long as this is slowly faded out when he is fully toilet trained. This happy state might be quite some way off yet as toilet training can be a slow process.

ENVIRONMENTAL

ACTION Now that your baby is on the way to learning how to crawl and to get about by himself, we can draw his attention to some other clues that will help him identify parts of his home—the lino in the kitchen, differences in carpet textures in different rooms. Let him have more experiences of kitchen things and what goes on there—potatoes with their peel, potatoes without their peel, let him help with the stirring, by putting things in saucepans, by having a chance to put his hands in flour, sugar, dried fruit, with the opportunity to taste and smell. You can show him how to pour some dry things out of one container into another—'kitchen time' should be something he enjoys.

ACTION In the sitting room (or wherever he has his play periods), show him how to creep or crawl off his play rug, say to the window (light is often the first thing they move towards), or to a chair, eventually to each part of the room so that he begins to have an idea of what is 'out there' before he actually goes by himself.

ACTION It is time he was encouraged to notice things that are outdoors—the differences between grass and paving stones or whatever there is in the garden. He should be given flowers to smell, sticks and stones (not small ones), dry leaves and all sorts of things that are around to feel and explore. If you can tape record some bird songs, you can let him hear these when he is outside.

And when you have him out in the pram, do not forget to run down slopes and 'puff' up slopes—these are experiences he will feel and later recognise when he is walking. When it is windy, let him have a plastic windmill on a stick to feel going round. When you meet people, make sure they know to give him the 'hallo' sign so that he knows they are there; encourage them to bend down and talk to him and touch him. And if he gets impatient because you are standing chatting, here is yet another chance to use the sign for 'wait'.

91

Stage 5

INTRODUCTION

This is the stage when all those motor skills which have led up to the deaf/blind child being able to move about by himself are consolidated. Now he must learn new skills necessary to the acquisition of the ability—possessed by man alone—to walk in an upright position. He has to learn to get up on to his feet, to stand and to walk with support from us and from things in his environment. It is perhaps one of the most demanding periods for parents, for much of the encouragement and incentive will need to come from them. If the child is active and motivated, he will require a lot of attention if his exploration is to provide information as well as increased motor ability. If he is passive and not too well motivated, we shall have to create inviting situations to stimulate him to move and learn, as well as go with him all the time.

This is the stage when a child begins to ask 'what' questions at every turn because of his interest in what he sees and what we tell him. We must assume that, when our deaf/blind child touches things or brings them close to his eyes, he too is asking this question and we must make sure we provide him with the answer. For instance, the seeing/hearing child taken shopping sees all the goodies, hears Mummy ask for the items, sees what the words she says mean, sees the exchange of money and knows that the purchases come home with them. How often did I take Bunty into a shop in the pram, buy something, put it in the basket and return home without a word or sign to her—I shudder to think how often! As far as possible, do let your deaf/blind child know what is going on around him. It will not be meaningful to him the first time, perhaps not the twentieth time, but only if he *has* the experience can things possibly ultimately be remembered, recognised and understood. It is only by knowing 'what is there' will he want to know 'what it is', 'what it is for' etc., *and* 'what *else* is there'. Repetition, however boring to you, is vital; again and again we must feed in information that is relevant to his stage of development.

In their book (see Appendix 3), McInnes and Treffrey suggest we keep in mind the word KISS—*keep it short and simple*. This applies not only to the amount of information and guidance we give the child, but to the signed and spoken sentences we use to put over the information. The signs I have suggested you should introduce are those most likely to be meaningful at each stage in relation to the child's own experiences. If he is responding well, you can introduce others of your own choice, so long as these are connected with something that you know, through your own careful observations, is understood by him. You must keep a note of these when you have started to use them so that everyone concerned with the care of the child also uses them. Equally so, the input of speech phrases must be consistent—it's no good calling the midday meal·dinner one day and lunch the next, or saying 'Go to the toilet' one time and 'Sit on the potty' the next. You must decide on the phrase you use and then stick to it until such time as communication is established and the child understands that all things have names and wants to know these.

Auditory input must not be restricted to speech only. Environmental sound—noise—is very much part of all our lives. We cannot ignore it, indeed it is imperative that we do not in the interests of safety (e.g. the fire alarm). So make sure you are always drawing the deaf/blind child's attention to sounds, what makes them and what they signify.

Up to now, communication for the deaf/blind child has been between him and another person. Has there been an opportunity for him to be aware that all people communicate with each other—that Mum can speak/sign to Dad and vice versa? Have you ever thought how much the seeing/hearing child learns incidentally by just overhearing the conversations of others—and that we continue to 'eavesdrop' for information this way all our lives? If there is sufficient vision, Mum and Dad (and others) must sign to each other where the deaf/blind child can see them and, if vision is too poor, put his hand on Mum's throat when she talks to Dad and then on Dad's when he replies. At this stage we want the child to become aware that everyone communicates—it is preparation for the time, a considerable way ahead as yet, he will be able to interpret and join in with group conversation.

I am sure by now you are able to see separately the various types of skills which we need to help the deaf/blind child develop. However, it is very important that none of us relies on any one skill; we are always using several together, depending on the specific situation. We bring these together—integrate them—to obtain maximum information from the environment, and we also combine several skills in order to respond, such as the co-ordination between hand and eye that allows us to write. This integration is vital. First we need to separate out the elements (as we have done) and now we need to look at an event as a whole, seeing what skills are involved but also asking ourselves if we could have added anything that would have made the experience more valuable. For example, if we are encouraging the child to bang a drum, we can also, without distracting him from the main objective, use this as a visual training exercise if we move the drum slightly sometimes, so that he has to look to see where to bang. Likewise, if he is standing against a chair, attract his attention visually to something bright and move this so that in order to see it he has to adjust his body and his balance (look round without falling down!). Try *now* to see what opportunities play offers for using as many skills as possible, rather than looking at play as a means of exercising a particular skill.

The Programme: Stage 5

ACTION Be aware of the need for balance between the togetherness you must have in order to share information/ activities and the risk of unknowingly being over-protective.

WHY If we want to encourage independence, we must—now the child is beginning to move about by himself—make him aware of things that may be harmful. We must find a clue that will warn him, accompany this with the sign 'No' and an appropriate word spoken sharply, e.g. 'fire', of which we cannot give the child the direct experience—touching the fireguard should be matched with the sign for 'No' and the word 'Hot'.

ACTION Observe your baby's reaction to strangers: it is quite normal for children about this time to show an awareness of the difference between familiar and unfamiliar adults. It is a good sign if this is seen in the deaf/blind child. Nevertheless, he should be encouraged through Mummy to 'explore' the new person. If that person has prepared for the encounter by having an interesting identity 'signal' and can play with the child an activity which it is known he enjoys and recognises, it should help him to learn to be friendly.

Observe your baby's reactions to being in a strange place. Is he interested or afraid? Does he cling to you or begin to explore by himself? If the latter, does he recognise familiar objects (chairs, tables) and does it take him long to 'know' where things are? Watching your child in new situations will give you lots of clues as to the way in which he is learning and, if he is not learning by himself, he needs you to give him the clues that help him identify the new situation (e.g. those things that are common to all sitting rooms, all gardens, all kitchens and so on). If it is necessary to take him and leave him somewhere new, take his play rug to create a familiar spot from which to begin to come to terms with the new.

ACTION It is now time, providing you feel your little one definitely recognises yours and his Daddy's special signals, to give him the means of using your relationship names. If when he touches your special signal (brooch, tiepin or whatever) you fingerspell 'Mum' or 'Dad', as appropriate on to his hand and then, taking his hand, fingerspell the word on to your hand, you are giving him the means to initiate communication, and making the first step towards symbolism. He has been able to give you body movements to tell you the kind of activity he wants you to play; he has moved on to 'you play me' (touching the person equalling 'you') and now he can advance to 'Mum play me'—the

95

importance of this being that it leads towards when *Daddy* can say to the child 'Mum play (with) you' and the child makes a request to *Daddy* that he wants 'Mum to play with him'. For a long time yet, communication will have to be related to the concrete, that which is there for the child actually to experience through touch or use of residual vision and hearing. Ultimately we want him to learn that these symbols (words or signs) can be used to refer to things whether they are present or not, and to use them to express his needs or thoughts, to use them to reason with, to recall past experiences and to be able to plan for the future. There are body signs for Mum and Dad, and in some cases touching a certain part of the body is used to indicate who a person is, but since ultimately a great many names (people, countries, places etc.) form part of our language system and will need to be finger-spelt, the introduction of simple spelt words seems appropriately begun at this stage. Remember, that for the deaf/blind child, fingerspelt letters are not letters to him, but a sequence or pattern of sensations received on his hand. A chart for finger-spelling is in Appendix 8—it is easy to learn and it is both fun and advisable to practise it amongst the family members. When you can both use and receive it efficiently, it acquires a rhythm of its own which will be detected by the deaf/blind child and could also alert him as to the identity of the person communicating with him.

New signs

ACTION I would suggest that you now introduce the following.

1. Sit down: hands slightly over each other, palms down, press down a couple of times. Initially do this when the child is close enough to have his hands touch the thing he is to sit on so that he can associate the two.

Sit down

Stand up

96

2. Stand up: palms of the adult's hands underneath the child's hands which are then moved in an upwards direction.

These signs can be used within a motor/fun activity shared by you and they provide preparation for the time (probably in Stage 6) when you can use them for a command to which he can respond without help.

3. Want: child's hand, palm upward, is moved forward from the chest.
4. Do: similar to the sign for 'finish', except that the lower hand is closed as well as the upper.
5. Give: is the 'want' sign in reverse.

These three verb signs allow us to begin to use simple three-word sentences so that we are following the normal developmental sequence (i.e. from the single word to the two-word sentence and now to that of three to four words).

If we add:

6. Spoon: a scooping movement upwards towards the face with one hand—this movement starting from the cupped palm of the other hand,
7. Biscuit: child taps elbow,

we can make sentences such as:

Child: 'I want (a) biscuit (to) eat.'

Mother: 'Mummy give you (a) biscuit.'

Want

Do

Give

97

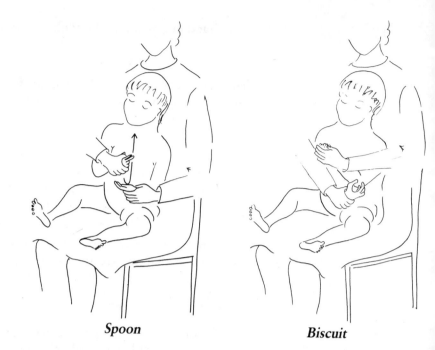

Spoon   *Biscuit*

These are suggestions—the important thing is to begin to expand communication in the natural way, that is, in sentences. If the child only learns the names of things, he is not learning language. All children go through a stage of 'telegraphese' before they use the full grammatical structure, and they make many grammatical mistakes along the way. Give the deaf/blind child the sentence, but accept approximations from him (with great joy). Introduce one at a time and, remember, signs must be felt many times before they will be remembered and associated with the object or action to which they refer.

VOCALISING

ACTION If imitation of vowel sounds is progressing well, begin to give your baby the feel of some of the consonants (his hand on the appropriate part of your face or throat):

m hand on your lips which are closed inwards with no air coming through.
p hand on your lips first closed inwards then opened to let out a puff of air which is felt on the child's hand.
b hand on your lips closed outwards and opening to let air out slowly.

Then add a vowel sound after a consonant (ah, oo, ou, ee, eh etc.), letting the child feel you making the change in shape of your face and mouth as it occurs. Very gradually, quicken up the change from the consonant to the vowel so that the sounds blend, e.g. you will be making the sounds 'me' 'ba' etc. You can also progress to making the vowel sound before the consonant, e.g. 'up' etc. Remember, you *must* have his attention when you are doing these exercises; keep the duration of the exercise short. Where these sounds occur in any of the special phrases you use, draw his attention to them by putting his hand to your face.

WHY He may make some of these sounds (and others) quite naturally but not necessarily deliberately—it is making them deliberately in recognition of their similarity to the speech sounds we make when talking to him that leads to him using speech sounds in context.

ACTION Watch to see if there is excessive use of any self-initiated sounds that the child makes a habit of using and might be using as a block against listening and which will therefore cause him to fail to appreciate sounds as a means of communication. Such sounds are often very unpleasant to the listener, and the child is well aware of this and can learn to use them to avoid contact. If the sounds the deaf/blind child hears are interesting and meaningful, he will listen; if he is rewarded when he makes pleasant sounds and is made to realise that we too make these sounds (and others), this kind of problem should not occur. It is often the result of lack of auditory input in the very early days.

ACTION Because the production of speech sounds depends on complex manipulation of the muscles of the mouth, jaw, lip and tongue, spending a few minutes each day helping your child to exercise these parts can be helpful. You may have to let him feel *you* doing them, and perhaps doing a little gentle manipulation of his face, in order that he knows what you want of him. The following are some ideas.

> Put your tongue out.
> Put your tongue out and waggle it.
> Blow up your cheeks and 'pop' them.
> Put something sweet/tasty on various parts of his lips and show him how to lick it off.
> Gently put against his lips things that contrast, e.g. something warm/cold, wet/dry, smooth/rough.

(*Moto-kinesthetic Speech Training* by Young and Hawk and *Motoric Aids to Perceptual Training* by Chaney and Kephart have many useful suggestions in this area.)

LISTENING ACTION Show your baby how to take turns at using sound makers: you shake the bell (making sure you have alerted him to the fact that this is what you are going to do), stop shaking it, give him time to appreciate that the sound has stopped, then show him how to take his turn at shaking it and to listen to it. Use the phrase 'Listen, (name) listen'. When he seems to understand this procedure, you each have a similar noise maker—let him operate his freely but keep drawing his attention to listening to yours while you hold his still for him. You can play this game with any instrument or noise-making toy which he can learn to use for himself, e.g. a drum, strum guitar strings, zylophone, maracca, ridged block of wood or fluted pelmet to rub with a stick or thimble.

Sounds should be quite loud to begin with, but after a while try reducing and see if you can determine how quiet it has to be for him not to hear it.

ACTION Draw his attention to more environmental sounds—get him to feel/listen to such things as the hair dryer, radio, door knocker, hoover, and try to get over to him what they are used for, how you use them and so on.

MOTOR DEVELOPMENT

ACTION Encourage your baby to crawl to a chair, show him how to sit back on his knees and then to rise into a kneeling position. Put his hand on to the seat where you have placed a favourite toy. When he has learned this part of the procedure, move the toy a little further back where he can just touch it, but not grasp it. Holding his hand firmly on to the seat, show him how to put the other hand beside it, to put his weight on to one knee and lift his body to stand on the other foot, then to pull himself to stand on both feet in order to obtain the toy. He may do all this quite naturally, but if not, showing him how to shift his weight may help. When he can stand leaning on to a chair or holding on to something to keep the upright position, show him how to reverse the process by touching his left foot with the toy to encourage him to release the hold of his left hand and bend down to reach it. When he does this, show him how to bend the left knee and shift his weight to allow him to get to the kneeling position. Lots of children just plop down on to their bottoms in order to get from standing to sitting, and you can take advantage of situations (standing holding on to the rail of a cot or playpen if used) which allow him to have this kind of experience.

Gross motor

ACTION Continue to encourage crawling, enlarging his experience of surfaces and also now providing obstacles for crawling over, round and under, e.g. lilo, foam rubber, pillows, mats with different textures, artificial grass, polystyrene wedges put together to provide an up and down course, and so on.

ACTION With his back to you, have him stand with his feet on yours while you walk, rocking a little from side to side so that he begins to learn about weight shifting—you can do this to music to vary the experience. Encourage him to shift his weight from foot to foot when he is standing holding on to a chair or small table and, when he can, show him how to use this action to cruise round the low table by moving sideways. Give him some support at the hips to begin with.

ACTION Walk him between two people holding his hands, reminding him by a little extra pull on his hands of the need to shift his weight. Help him to push around a weighted trolley, gradually lessening the amount of support you give him. To add to his incentive to move about by himself, give him periods in the baby-walker and note whether he is becoming aware of the position of things around him as he recognises what he bumps into—i.e. is beginning to get a mental map of his immediate environment.

ACTION Encourage your baby to touch and explore the furniture he uses as an aid to walking and, as he increases his proficiency, arrange things so he can move from one piece of furniture to the next. If you do this now, you are preparing for the next stage when by moving furniture just that little bit further apart he can be tempted to take the necessary step without holding on.

A good game at this stage is 'Ring-a-ring of roses' as this involves side-walking. Also, when your baby is confident in the standing position, you can use a hoop of which he holds one side and you the other, encouraging him to move forward. Alternatively, you can use a piece of broom handle which he holds onto. If you can organise something like the parallel bars used in physiotherapy, this provides practice.

Balance is basic to standing and it is usually necessary for the child to have a fairly wide stance to begin with.

In all these activities the child may need to be shown exactly what he has to do—even to the manipulation of the limbs—and may need the experience with and through you many times before being asked to try on his own.

Fine motor

ACTION Having learned to reach, grasp and use his hands as tools to operate on things in his environment, he now needs to learn the various ways in which he can use these 'tools'. What he needs now are opportunities to poke, roll, tear, push, squeeze, pat, bang, swipe, rub, punch and to pick up things of various sizes right down to very small items. Playdoh, paper, large Lego bricks and other construction toys which can be fixed together and pulled apart easily are all useful. Much of the information about these actions you will convey to your baby through your own hands as you show him what to do using the 'hands on' position, but some will come from the position and movements of your whole body against his. For instance, if together you have rolled some Playdoh into a long sausage and then, holding each end together, you pull it apart into two, you can convey a lot of information about 'pulling' by pretending it is very hard and moving sharply when it does come apart so that he is aware of the feeling of the spring that occurs—if the word 'pull' accompanies the action, it provides a good auditory input. Likewise, when you press together the two bits of Playdoh you now have with the appropriate effort needed and accompany this with the word 'squeeze' in a fairly high-pitched tone, you are conveying a lot of information. Take advantage of any opportunities offered within everyday routine situations to practise the above fine motor skills, giving emphasis to the direction and effort in the movement and naming the action. These skills precede such activities as sorting, stacking, threading etc.

PLAY

ACTION If tracking up and down, to the sides and across the midline is now achieved, diagonal tracking (from corner to corner) would be the next stage. A large square piece of cardboard with a circular slit cut out of it around which a torch travels will encourage smooth tracking movement.

ACTION Continue to observe your baby's response to colour—put several similar objects in line in front of him, each of a different colour, and notice if he regularly picks up the same one. Are his favourite toys similar in colour? Encourage him to 'scan' (an important visual skill) by spacing out several toys on a table and getting him to look from one to the other (using a torch if necessary) before making a choice as to which one he wants.

ACTION As mobility increases, more of your child's time will be spent exploring his environment—if this excites him, he may be less inclined to want to sit and play with you or with toys. However, it is a good plan to keep two or three short periods at regular times during the day when you do sit down and play together.

WHY All children need to sit to learn, and with the deaf/blind child the habit cannot be encouraged too soon and, when it does become habit, it should be maintained. Once these children do become mobile they often become hyperactive, moving from object to object and not stopping long enough to learn anything about it. The length of these play periods must depend on the length of the child's interest in what you are doing, and this may vary from day to day. It is most important that you recognise when he is getting bored and either try a new activity or alter the focus of that you are engaged upon. Also it is important that when the child's interest is held, you do not change the activity for the sake of changing it, but rather see how you can extend the scope of the activity so that you are progressing towards the next stage.

ACTION The following are some activities you might now play together.

1. Show him how to find things:
(a) under cartons,
(b) in a pocket sewn on to an apron or cushion.
2. Show him how to
(a) fit a wooden circle into a formboard,
(b) fit a peg into a board with just the one hole in it,
(c) push a small object through a large ring.
Praise him when he succeeds and make sure you show him the result of what he has done. Provide tactile clues by covering items with different textured materials.

3. Show him how to play with wind-up toys that vibrate, make a noise, or move along; ratchet toys, musical roundabouts, friction toys, spinning tops (the press-down type).

4. Introduce more action rhymes, but keep up those already known. Pat-a-cake is a nice one to encourage anticipation, imitation and body awareness. Observe whether, if you alter a bit or leave out a bit of a sequence, your baby is aware of this.

5. Make a chute out of the cardboard insides of kitchen foil or clear wine-making tubing; show him how to post things down and listen for the sound they make as they fall into a metal box or tin.

ACTION While one would expect crawling about and pulling himself up to standing to be the major preoccupation of the deaf/blind child at this stage when we are not actually playing with him, we should still be encouraging him to find and explore new objects which we will place so that he comes across them as he moves around. The following are some of the things which you can make or purchase quite cheaply and which might catch his interest.

Coloured popcorns in a bag.
Six-sided photo holder—different textures in place of photos.
Transparent pop bottles quarter-filled with coloured water.
Various coloured tinsels.
Long balloon with peas in it—half blown up so he can hold the empty end.
Plastic carton with clothes pegs clipped on to it, which he takes off and puts on.
RNIB Bleep ball (No. 9201).
Box of bits—hair rollers, plastic egg cups, pipe cleaners etc.
Stick refractive paper (which you can buy by the metre from Paperchase, 213 Tottenham Ct. Road, London WC1) on margarine tops (or similar) to make shiny toys (also mobiles). You can also use sequins.
Feely caterpillar—circles of different texture material joined in pairs and stuffed with old tights, join together with Velcro, i.e. velvet to velvet, so each has different sides.
Matchboxes covered with different textured material—with sweet inside (if he likes sweet things) to encourage him to learn how to open. Start with the large-sized matchboxes.
Using $\frac{3}{4}$-inch plywood, make several play boards as follows.

1. A wobble board—fix 4″ to 8″ plastic-covered flexible curtain wire and attach various-sized beads etc. to the top.

2. A 'switch' board—fix various kinds of switches. If these can also operate a small light, and each switch has a different colour (fairy light-type bulbs), they are greatly enjoyed and can be useful as a reward.

3. A board with rings attached to it so that you can hang various objects on to it and change these easily.

4. A board covered with material on to which three or four pockets have been fixed into which you can put things for the child to find. Later these can have zips to undo or buttons to unfasten—in fact all kinds of different fastenings that will help practise for being able to manage those on his clothes.

If the child is at a table playing with these, then a small wedge stuck to the back at the top raising it to slanting position can be helpful. An easel-type back to the board may make it easier to play with when the child is on the floor.

ROUTINES
Feeding

ACTION Your baby should now be ready to be encouraged to: (1) lift and hold a cup by himself—show him how to tilt to drain and then make sure he puts it down on the table (keep the amount in the cup small), and (2) help himself to a favourite food.

If possible, let him sit at the table with you and eat with the family—mealtimes are sociable occasions and we must not deny the deaf/blind child the experience which he will get from the general chatter and movement going on.

Encourage him to finger feed and pull off his own bib. Let him feel his milk being poured into his cup and show him how, by using his finger down the inside of the cup, he can feel how much has gone in and, when he has drunk it, that there is now none there. Decrease the amount of help you give to feeding himself with a spoon in the following stages:

release his hand before the spoon goes into his mouth,
after the spoon is filled,
before the spoon is filled,
only put the spoon in his hand,
let him look for the spoon and pick it up himself,
prompt only by touching his elbow.

Give plenty of help in scooping and finding the food in the dish because this is difficult where vision is very poor—if the spoon keeps coming up empty, he could think his plate is empty. Popping a little bit on the spoon without him knowing often helps at this stage. There are plate surrounds which prevent food from being pushed off the edge of a plate, but a bowl (not too rounded) is better while the amount of food is comparatively small.

Food should generally by now be roughly mashed up, but meat needs to be well cut up.

ACTION He should now be beginning to learn more about food and where it comes from, e.g. before breakfast let him feel his empty bowl, then the cereal box (nice for sound and vibration when shaken), help you to tip it up and pour some into his bowl (tip over one of his hands so he is aware of what is happening as a result of tipping the box). Let him feel the milk jug and help him tip some on to the cereal (feeling how much with his finger down inside of bowl). Let him learn how to sprinkle on the sugar. If you have a different kind of cereal, let him help you to serve yours—*and* offer him a taste, for with almost all children this is a good way of getting them to try something different. Do not try to do all the above sequence at once. Take one thing first and when he understands and can do this, tackle the next stage, and so on.

Let him feel the loaf of bread, the cutting action of the knife with his hand over yours and then give him a slice. In other words, whenever there is an opportunity to give him information about food and mealtimes, take advantage of it—food is important to him (and good eating habits a blessing to mums), and the more we can interest him in it the better.

Washing   ACTION With one of the commercially made 'steps' (Mothercare) or, better still, make one yourself, help the child to stand to the basin and take him through the hand-washing routine—letting him feel you turn on the tap with one hand while his other hand feels the water coming out. Put in the plug together, find the soap, rub on, rinse off, pull out the plug and make him feel the water disappearing and, when it is all gone, give him the sign for 'all gone'. Keep his towel in a place where he can reach it, help him find it and (standing behind in 'hands-on' position) show him how to dry his hands. Gradually back-chain this procedure so that the child begins to do it himself. Add face washing when hand washing is achieved.

WHY Now that the child is standing and is able to maintain this position, more and more activities come within his reach. We do not need to wait until he can stand alone; so long as we support him in the standing position (or he is leaning on a support, e.g. the basin), we can increase his experiences leading to self-care, at the same time strengthening the muscles for standing.

Bathing   ACTION If you keep bath toys in a box or bag, you can let him stand against the bath and put them in the bath for himself. Keep his nightwear and towel somewhere outside the bathroom and before bathing take him to get these things—he needs to begin to learn that special things are kept in special places.

Continue the bath routine as before, encouraging him to do more of the washing, keep up the massage and body image awareness, letting him rub in the cream or powder when possible. Some of the action water toys in the toy list should now amuse him.

Dressing   ACTION Continue to back-chain your help in dressing and undressing—he will advance more quickly in undressing. Does he yet get any clues from feeling the texture and shape of a garment as to which part of his body it must go on, e.g. put his foot up if you give him his sock to feel?

When taking off his pants now (and nappy if he still wears one), stand him with his back to you, take his hands, put his thumbs round the elastic and help him push them down over his hips, put a little pressure on him with your body so that he bends his knees

105

a little and can lift each foot in turn to take the pants right off. Use the same procedure in reverse when putting his pants on, hooking the thumbs round the elastic to edge them over his hips and then moving his hands towards the centre back to pull up that last bit at the back.

WHY Now he is standing, you can be preparing him for the kind of movements he will need to make to go independently to the toilet once he is walking alone—some time ahead, but we cannot begin too early to introduce him to this kind of experience while giving him total support.

ACTION Put a tactile label of some sort on the back of his vests and pants to stress the difference between the back and front, and get the child into the *habit* of feeling for this before putting them on—the reason will become clear to him when he begins to dress himself. If he has sufficient vision, the label could be a coloured one.

Toiletting   ACTION It is best now to use one of the potties with a good back and front support. He should not need you to be quite so close to him now, but if he does not seem too happy to begin with, you could try putting the potty in a big cardboard box so that he can hang on to the sides or put a chair in front of him to hold on to.

If possible, leave off nappies during the day—awareness of toiletting needs seems to come more quickly when there is no nappy to catch it! Nappies tend to encourage children to walk with a wide gait after they have acquired balance and really no longer need to do this. The potty should be beginning to be used occasionally now, but if it is not, *do not worry*. Without visual and auditory clues in a situation where tactile clues are difficult (and not hygienic!), getting toilet trained is certain to take longer. Keep calm and let your child know when he pleases you by performing on the potty, but never make a fuss about accidents. Like feeding, this is a situation in which our anxiety to have our child conforming to what is socially acceptable is easily conveyed to the child and may, in turn, affect his ability to relax and respond. With some of these children there is an actual physical delay in the development of the control needed, and without this they cannot be expected to be toilet trained. For many deaf/blind children, helping to operate the loo flush and listening to the rushing water is a welcome reward for having used the potty.

ENVIRONMENTAL   ACTION Encourage him to:

follow you to other rooms by crawling—do not carry him anywhere he could crawl or walk with either one or both his hands held,

walk all round the beds and find the pillows—he can help you punch up the pillows when you are bed making,

rock from foot to foot to music—he can even do a little

'twisting' so long as it is rhythmic and not too fast,

begin to go up the stairs on hands and knees—only when you are with him,

go with you to the door when you greet visitors.

Try to let him know what you are doing and encourage him to imitate you, e.g. dusting a low table, brushing the carpet, holding on to the hoover etc.

ACTION Let him walk for short distances outside (one hand held or perhaps holding on to his pushchair). Encourage him to feel the fences and gates, low walls—things at his level along the street. Let him walk in the autumn leaves and puddles and draw his attention to what is happening. With you holding him, let him go on the park swings etc. And, when shopping, do not do what I did: make sure your child is well aware of the empty shopping bag when you go into the shop and let him help you put things into it as you buy them, as well as unpack them when you get them home.

INTRODUCTION

Stage 6

Now we come to what is a major goal for all children—the ability to walk on their own. The sheer physical ability required to do this may not be difficult for the deaf/blind child to acquire, but making full use of this new skill, improving it by use and developing those other upright motor skills which follow (running, jumping etc.) and, most important, using it to explore and learn about his environment, depends very much on the motivation within the child himself. Children enjoy physical activities for the joy of moving, but what they see and hear does provide the incentive for using and practising the skill automatically. Like communication, you do not teach it, you use it. Once walking is achieved, it is used as a means to an end. Our walking is purposeful, to get something, to go somewhere—if there is no need to walk, we sit down, lie down or do some other physical activity. Unless the deaf/blind child is motivated to walk as a means to an end, he will not necessarily take advantage of his new skill. *We* must see to it that walking is lots of fun and we must let him know how pleased we are with his achievement. We must also, particularly in the early stages, see that there is some tangible reward for having walked—if it has been to please us, we must give him a big hug, if he has walked to the toy corner, he must be given a toy, if he has made it to the kitchen, perhaps a biscuit or a taste of something he likes very much. If the deaf/blind child does not find that walking is useful to him, he has a tendency to sit, and sit and sit—if he wants something, once he can walk by himself, do not get it for him, encourage him to be independent.

Deaf/blind children often take a long time to progress from one stage to another. They seem to get stuck on a plateau despite our encouragement and, usually, just as we begin to despair, they take the new step forward and it is a big one. Learning has been taking place although this has not been obvious. As we have progressed through the stages of this programme we have been widening the child's horizons, asking a lot of him. Now, so much more becomes within his reach—we must be careful not to ask too much of him, not to overload him with information, not to confuse him. Only you, his parents, can judge the speed at which he can absorb new things and know when it is best to introduce them, can curb your natural enthusiasm and let the child dictate the pace. So long as there is progress, however small, there is no cause for anxiety. It is better if progress is being made across the board, in all areas—I thought Bunty's problems would be solved if she could communicate, but you cannot communicate unless you have something to communicate about and this requires that you can reach, know and understand your environment. You, as a family, are unique and your child's needs are unique to him—a programme such as this can only generalise, and it is for you to take from it what suits you and your child.

The Programme: Stage 6

RELATIONSHIP

Emotional and social development

Now that your child is increasing his awareness of the people around him, his environment and the daily pattern of his life, he is also discovering himself and his ability to act on his own. It is a frustrating time for most children, partly inherent in growing up, but particularly so for the deaf/blind child. He may indeed know what he wants and yet have no means of expressing himself other than appearing frustrated. He may want to handle things in his own way rather than follow our direction, and he needs this freedom, it is the basis for later independence and emotional stability. It is not at all easy to interpret these needs in the child, and it is very much a period of trial and error for parents and interveners. It is a time when attention-seeking behaviour increases and the child becomes aware of the significance of the adults in his life and the difference in their approach to him—how easily and when they will give in to his demands.

It may seem hard to say that you must be firm with a 'poor child' who is deaf/blind, but he of all children needs to have guidelines and limits drawn up for him. *Agreed* consistent responses from all members of the family will gradually help him to learn to control his own behaviour and to reconcile his own desires with the demands made on him from the environment.

Frustration can lead to aggression, and if the child learns he can get what he wants by being aggressive, this behaviour will continue. If we punish him, he has at least got our attention—if this satisfies him he will keep up the aggressive behaviour. Unfortunately there are no magic answers to this problem. How *you* deal with it, if it arises, depends on the socially accepted mores within your family and it requires a delicate balance between permissiveness and restraint. If you can anticipate the situation which leads to aggressive behaviour and prevent it happening, this is one solution.

COMMUNICATION

ACTION Within the family circle you may now find it possible to associate other members' special touch signals with a finger-spelt name, nickname or shortened version of the full name. This is an individual choice, but one idea might be:

for Grandma spell   g-m u m   or   g- m a
for Grandpa spell   g-d a d   or   g- p a

Once begun, keep it up, and do not miss any opportunity to use it. Remember, when you have spelt it on to his hand, show him how to spell it on to your hand and on his own hand so that there is feedback.

109

WHY Remember, it is not enough to teach him the signs, he must also be learning how to make them for himself.

New signs

ACTION Introduce the following new signs.

1. More: clenched left hand moves to meet palm of right hand at the midline.
2. Up: index finger of one hand pointed upwards.
3. Down: index finger of one hand pointed downwards.
4. In: index finger of one hand placed in circle made by thumb and index finger of the other hand.
5. On: right hand, palm upwards, brought down on to the left palm.

These are five words which you will find occurring frequently in routine and play situations. As always, introduce slowly—do not overload so that your child becomes confused. On the other hand, if his awareness of certain objects or events is evident and he appears to have a good understanding of their meaning, you can introduce the signs for them. Only you, by observing him carefully, can decide which and at what stage new signs can be started, but from now on it has to be a slow, steady build up of input and a constant encouragement of the child to use what he knows *because it is useful to him*—the *need* to communicate (which we must often engineer) is the best possible incentive to communicating. As his awareness of the usefulness of communi-

Child's own signals

cating grows, the child may devise some of his own signals. For instance, if his coat is fastened with a zip, he may well indicate his desire to go out by going through the motions of zipping something up, or perhaps he will make a throwing-up movement with his hands to indicate he wants his ball. You need to watch carefully for such signals and respond to his requests—at the same time giving him his sign together with the correct one so that he can learn that they mean the same thing.

VOCALISING

ACTION If imitation is progressing well, you can introduce some new blends. For the child with useful vision these can be related to pictures of animals (not to toy models). Although we might think we could use toy models for the child with poor sight or blind, in no way could he relate the models with the real thing in the way that we can. These blends, which are recommended by Professor Barbara Franklin, lend themselves later on to little picture stories which will help memory and sequencing: wa wa= duck, wo wo=dog, mieu=cat, baa=sheep, moo=cow. The phrase to use is 'The duck *says* wa wa' **not** 'This is a duck', for the blend equals the sound the animal makes and is not its name, which will come later. It is the ability to blend the sounds that we are aiming for at this stage, nothing else. Accept any approxima-tions of these sounds with pleasure and watch out now for any sounds which your baby makes in context which might be the beginning of real words. Sometimes these children are better able

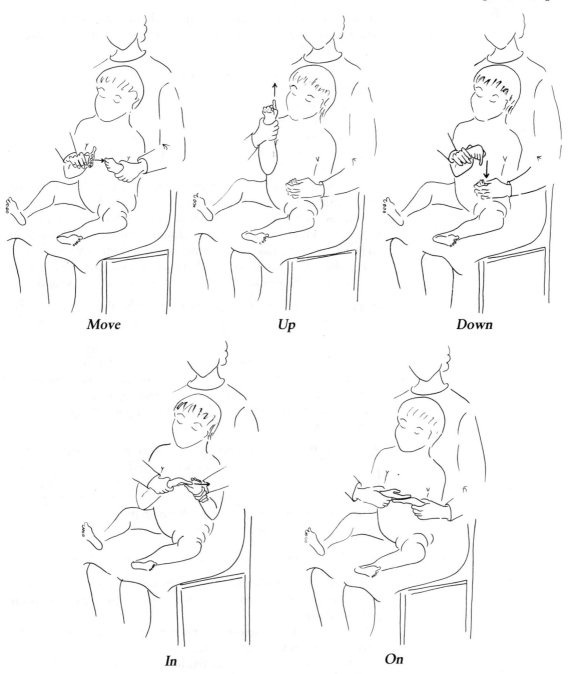

Move   *Up*   *Down*

In   *On*

to recognise a spoken word once they know the sign for it—these are often the words to which they first try to give voice.

Today there are toys (and indeed some computer programs) which, when you make a sound, light up, and this is a splendid reward for a good attempt at imitating sounds.

LISTENING   ACTION Continue to play listening games and remember that on these occasions you must be in a quiet room and not be

111

disturbed. You must make sure the child is in a position to hear and is attending. Give clear sounds and give him time to respond. See if:

1. he can copy you if you bang the drum
(a) just once or lots of times,
(b) slowly/quickly,
(c) loudly/quietly,

(he must have the tactile clues and you must show him exactly how he must handle the drumstick in order to create the differences);

2. each time you bang the drum, he can put a brick in a box (or some similar activity which he enjoys and which is related to a sound). At first he must be able to see you bang the drum, then see if he can do it only by hearing the sound. Some children latch on to other clues such as the movement of your arm or sleeve as you make the bang, so in the final stages of this game use a tape recording of the sounds to which he is expected to respond.

It can take a long time for children to learn the above games, so be patient and introduce them regularly amongst other activities with you.

WHY (1) Contrasts highlight differences and this is what we want the child to become aware of. (2) This game is often used by audiologists to test whether a child is hearing or not and, when they use properly calibrated toys or instruments, gives some idea of the range of the hearing loss.

ACTION If you think your child is beginning to listen to and recognise some of the phrases which you have used by now hundreds of times in routine and play situations, try him out: say the phrase without the sign and see if he makes the right response. *However*, whether or not he does, keep up the signing, which is as yet *his* only means of communication.

ACTION To encourage listening, the following toys are useful.

Fisher-Price records and various types of players—the child can insert for himself and push the start. There is plenty of vibration and repetition.

A board with various sound makers fixed to it—bicycle bell, horn or siren, telephone bell etc.

Toys played with on a tin baking tray give increased sound feedback. Also, if you make a small screen which can enclose the area in front of the child as he plays, this helps to make sound reverberate. This could be used either on the floor or on the table and it could be covered with a reflective material.

MOTOR   ACTION
1. Encourage your child to walk both indoors and outdoors with only one hand held. If he tends to swing forwards or

backwards to begin with, give a little support to the shoulder of the hand not being held. Holding one of his hands encourages him to move with the other against the wall. Lessen the support to the hand you are holding—at this stage it is for balance, later he will use his hand on the wall for exploration and information.

2. With you kneeling behind him holding him at the hips, show him how to shift weight from side to side, forward and backwards, so that he is taking steps in all directions. Also in this situation show him how to 'fall' should he lose his balance: push down so he bends his knees, and his hands and bottom reach the floor together and he 'falls' backwards; push forward the hips so he will tip forward and catch himself with his hands.

3. Help him practise getting up from kneeling by pulling gently on his hands and, when he is in the upright position, encourage him to take a few steps towards you. Gradually lessen the support you give him as he takes these steps, but still hold both his hands.

4. As for (3) but with a second person behind him who supports him at the hips as soon as he is upright. You loose his hands, the second person releases his hold giving the child the smallest nudge forward, you catch his hands as he comes forward. Make a fun game of this and, as he gets used to it, gradually widen the gap between you and the other person, so that the child is encouraged to make a step to reach the support of your hands.

5. Some deaf/blind children walk by themselves in no time at all, others take a long time. *When* your child *can* walk a few steps between two people, turn him round when he reaches you and let him learn to walk to the other person. This experience of turning round when upright is very important as it requires skilful balance.

6. Balancing skills can be improved by helping the child to walk along a balance board (both hands held to begin with, then one—alternate sides, of course). The board should be wide enough for him to stand on comfortably with both feet together, about 2 inches thick and 7 to 8 feet long. Initially it should be placed on the floor and the child made to feel it with his hands, shown how to step on to it and again feel his feet on it with his hands and feel its relationship to the floor. When he has walked to the end, make a big thing of jumping him off. Once he has got the idea, you can raise the board off the ground a bit more, then a bit more—always letting the child know the change that has been made. Gradually you lessen the support you give him as he learns to use his own muscles to balance.

7. Organise a little motor 'course'—in the garden or, on rainy days, perhaps in the hall. In addition to the balance board you could have a large cardboard box to crawl through, a low stool to step up on to and off which the child could be jumped, and ending with, say, a go on a rocking horse. In the garden you could link these things with a slide, a climbing frame, a swing and possibly a small trampoline (sunk into the ground preferably). The child must have plenty of information about what you want him to

do—do not *take* him through an activity, *show* him how to do it (there is a difference).

8. This is the time to introduce the little trike (and other vehicles) which the child can sit on and move himself along with his feet.

9. Outside, give him experience such as walking up and down slopes, up and down curbs. If there is a grassy slope in the park, show him how to come down on his bottom or, if he likes it, to roll down.

10. Arrange a rope round the grass area in the garden and show him how to follow this holding on with both, then one, of his hands. When he is confident, you can have things hung on to the rope for him to find or you can give him a ball (or toy) to carry to the end and there put it into a box. Just following a rope will become boring once he can do it—so provide some incentives so that he gets as much walking practice as possible.

11. Wall-walking round rooms at home (if it is possible) encourages both walking and exploration. It depends on the facilities your home offers, but the kind of thing to encourge this activity would be a small wooden slat fixed round the wall at the child's hand height. Carefully fixed, its removal and hiding the screw holes could be easily dealt with when no longer required. This rail could be covered with a textured or bright material, different in different rooms, and where wall furniture interrupts this, the child has to learn to use this and then finds his way back to the rail again. This is not an essential training item, but it is a way of enticing the child to move and to explore. You could hang different things from the rail for him to find. Alternatively, if you could have a rail round one room only, you could attach to this (with Velcro) a variety of textured strips, e.g. herbs, rice, pasta, cotton wool, fur, sponge, foil, rubbers, polystyrene, tissues which have been scented, sandpaper, stones, shells—just to give you a few ideas! Another similar exercise involves following a line made with masking tape which goes round furniture, over obstacles, into different rooms and perhaps could end up in the toybox where the child can find his favourite toy.

WHY All the foregoing ideas are intended to encourage the child not only to walk, but to want to walk. It is important that he gets his confidence through carefully thought-out progressive lessening of the help we give him, that we show him there are ways of getting about without our help and that, when he is ready, we let him go by himself.

ACTION The following exercises are useful now and can be made part of your play together.

Supine: encourage him to raise one leg and then the other.
Standing: reach up on tiptoe; hold out arms at shoulder height and bend elbows.

Body image and imitation

Hand skills related to finger spelling: put index fingers together; touch index fingers to the tip of each finger and the thumb of the other hand.

If you tap a part of his body, see if he can tap the same spot himself (having been shown what you want him to do). You can rub the body part rather than tap it if this gets a better response.

PLAY

ACTION While it is important that the deaf/blind child becomes familiar with his toys, explores them fully, experimenting with them in a variety of ways, comparing them with those that are similar or different in some aspects, it is also necessary to watch that he does not become bored with them. Having something ready that is new and will stimulate both his interest and exploration is always advisable. Here are some ideas.

1. Play boards:
one with a set of door fastenings, e.g. a handle, a knob that turns, a hook and eye, a button catch, a latch and so on;

Fine motor skills

another with inserts over which there are hinged doors and which can be opened to see/find inside pictures, textures, raised outlines of familiar things, shapes stuck on (can be changed from time to time to keep interest);

another with just hooks on it together with a box of things he can hang on the hooks, take them off and change them around for himself.

Touch

2. Using a medium-sized cardboard box with two holes in it, show the child how to put his hands through and find some items related to daily routines—give him the signs for these when he finds them at first. If he gets good at it, give him the sign and see if he can find the object to which it relates (this is quite advanced).

Fine finger skills

3. Let him find and pick up small things such as Smarties, sultanas, Sugar-puffs etc., or get such things out of the bottom of a cup or carton.

4. Old catalogues make good playthings, particularly if there is some colour awareness.

5. If you do use rings on sticks or graded cups, remember size is a concept generally learned later on. Extract every other ring or cup to give more contrast between those he plays with and show him how to cup his hand round each to help him be aware of the size difference—vision being replaced by a skilful use of kinesthetic information. It is better to have him stack real things (plastic plates, saucers etc.) or to learn to put little plastic spoons in a small box and big ones in a bigger box. Use real-life things wherever possible.

6. Have a box of containers with pop-on tops; show him first how to pull these off and then how to replace them. Have another box of containers with screw tops which are only lightly put on—show him how to unscrew and get them off. Screwing on again is more difficult and he will need a lot of help to begin with. When you start, have only a few of each and of the same sort and

size; gradually increase the number of containers and use some different sizes—eventually you can mix both screw and pop-on tops for him to sort out, but take this progression very slowly.

7. If your child has some useful vision, you can show him how to hold a crayon (palmar grasp) and make big scribbles (black on yellow paper shows up best).

8. Show him how to unwrap things, then give him some odds and ends wrapped lightly in various kinds of paper.

There are a number of toys on the market these days which light up in one way or another: while these can be useful and amusing, guard against play with them for long periods lest they cause the child to become obsessive and stereotype in play. Light can be integrated into some toys as an incentive, for instance in the bottom of a shape posting box which then lights up each time a shape is successfully posted (the switch being operated by you as required).

There are also various vibratory toys, but these are only useful if they have some purpose, e.g. the muscle massager which has several different brushes which give the child different sensations and offer him the opportunity for choice.

Smell is also incorporated in books and toys these days, but for smell to be associated and remembered, it must be with the real thing, so these are of little use to the deaf/blind child at this stage.

If you are playing with your child in the 'hands on' position at a table, sit opposite a mirror and you will then be able to 'see' what he is doing as well as 'feel' it.

ROUTINES

Feeding

ACTION By now your little one should be on the way to feeding himself. Because feeding is so closely associated with the mother-figure, it is sometimes difficult for the child himself to accept the break in this tie—if he cannot see that we all do feed ourselves, he may feel hurt that mother is no longer prepared to feed him and so resist all efforts to get him to feed himself. Do not make a battle of it, but keep at it and withdraw your support gradually but surely. Food can probably now be chopped into small pieces rather than being mashed—meat is usually the greatest problem and may need to be very finely shredded still. Allow him to try new tastes—let him know first that you like whatever it is, let him smell it and feel it. If he rejects it without tasting, accept this—but offer it again on another occasion each time as he is likely to try eating it once it has become familiar.

Self-care

ACTION Begin involving him in what is going on at mealtimes. Let him learn how to help himself to things at table—vegetables, cakes, bread and butter etc. He can begin to use a plate at mealtimes: you can obtain special rims which fit round and prevent things from being pushed off the plate while he is learning. Show him how to find out what is on the plate, where it is (and when it is all gone) by running his spoon across the plate.

'Hands on', show him how to pour out his own milk. Only put a little in the jug to begin with (let him feel where the spout is) and as he holds this with one hand the other must be round the cup so that he can judge where the jug must be. The jug should rest on the cup and he should have one finger of the hand holding the cup down inside the cup so that he can feel the milk coming up in the cup and know when to stop pouring. (It is interesting that later on, when hot liquid is being poured into the cup, the deaf/blind learn to judge how much they have poured by feeling the rise of the warmth on the *outside* of the cup.) If he has sugar, he should be shown how to put this in the cup for himself and stir it up. Perhaps he might also learn with your help how to spread butter on bread—do not forget it is not just a matter of spreading, you have to let him feel the bread without the butter, the butter without the bread, and then the effect (taste also) of bringing them together.

When the meal is finished, let him (with help if necessary to begin with) carry a plate to the kitchen and put it into the bubbly washing-up water.

When he can walk reasonably well, he can be shown how to put the things on the table before the meal. If he has vision for colour, he could have his own set of things which are different from those of the other members of the family. If he needs tactile clues, glue a piece of string on the bottom of his plate, cup and spoon and show him how to feel for this to identify his things. You could also identify other people's things with different shapes in string— and, while this may seem unnecessary, the more we can encourage the child to be aware of the clues that are there for him to find, the more likely is he to develop the habit of looking for them for himself.

Bathing ACTION In the bath encourage him to do as much for himself as he can and to be as free as possible in the water—deaf/blind children generally love water, particularly pouring it over themselves. The bath is a good place for washing hair too. Involve him more and more in the preparation that goes on before the bath *and* in the clearing up that follows—he should be well able to put his dirty clothes in the basket and should be shown how to hang up the towel.

Washing ACTION Here again, encourage him to do as much for himself as possible, but supervise so that you are there to prompt (and see there are no floods!).

Dressing and undressing ACTION Watch for signs that he is beginning to know which item of clothing is going to be put on next and making the appropriate movements to take them off—this is described as 'assisting in dressing/undressing' and is a question often asked during an assessment. Put some kind of identifying mark on his shoe so that he can begin to learn which shoe goes on which foot. Let him help to get his coat and hat when going out and to put

117

them away when he comes in. Where possible, let him choose what he wants to wear—shoes or boots—given that you have provided him with some information that helps him make the right choice (he has been taken outside to feel the rain or snow, so needs boots).

Remember, learning how to dress and undress helps the child to learn about his own body, but body image activities also help him to learn about dressing and undressing.

Toiletting

ACTION Show him how to use and dispose of tissue hankies.

ACTION Little boys should stand to the toilet now. It should also be possible to begin the transition from the potty to the real toilet using a child seat and making sure that he has something on which to rest his feet while on the toilet, otherwise the feeling of insecurity will inhibit his ability to perform. He should be encouraged to push down his pants by himself and to complete the pulling up. Begin now to use the proper sign for 'toilet' in conjunction with the 'pants down' *signal*. This is done by putting the child's thumb between the 1st and 2nd fingers and, holding his hand in this position, give it a double shake.

Toilet

ACTION Now that he is walking, hand held or soon on his own, he can be involved in more of the daily routines that do not concern him so directly. Taking his plate from the table to the kitchen for washing up is an example, helping to put things away in their proper place afterwards is another. Break the tasks up into small steps to begin with and gradually build up to the whole task, e.g. carrying his plate only a few feet to begin with, putting just one clean spoon away in the drawer. Keeping the demands we make on the child quite small and letting him become familiar with each step before we ask more means that we must be clear in our own minds what is entailed in the task as a whole, that we plan the steps and, having begun, do our best to complete the programme. It may seem tedious, but the surer are the foundations laid by these simple tasks, the better will be the child's ability to paticipate in family life and, later, in life beyond the family.

ENVIRONMENT

Communication opportunities

ACTION He can now learn to take the cereal boxes to the breakfast table and take them to where they are kept afterwards. It does not matter if these are in a high cupboard—you will lift him up to reach them, and once he has tumbled to the routine, here is a natural opportunity for him to use the sign 'up'. Within the framework of all these routine situations there are many opportunities for communicating—do not miss them.

Self-identity

ACTION Once he can feed himself well, he could sit to the table with the rest of the family. Let him know that this is promotion: you sit on big chairs, now he is big enough to do the same. Have a special identifying tag on his chair so he knows where to sit.

ACTION Similar identity tags could be placed on the peg on

which his hat and coat are kept (low enough for him to use) and if there are other children in the family, on those things which are specially his. Becoming possessive is natural at this stage—we must help the deaf/blind child become aware that some things are his own.

ACTION Below are other things in which your child might be involved now.

In the garden with Daddy: feeling the grass long and then short when cut.

Cleaning the car with Daddy: feeling the water running over the car, then dry and shiny.

Helping Mummy to cook: putting ingredients together, stirring puddings, and tasting them, feeling the cake mixture in the patty tins before and after cooking.

If a deaf/blind child is not helped to be aware of what is going on around him, he will not learn about real life.

Outdoors ACTION Have a purpose in your daily walk and indicate this by signing or signals, for example:

posting a letter: the child can carry this to the letter box (he can also learn to collect the letters brought by the postman and take them to an adult),
shopping,
visiting a neighbour,
going to the park,
fetching children from school,
going swimming,
going on a bus.

Make him aware of the kerb before crossing a road and having crossed to the other side.

Take him out in the rain and the snow and make him aware of how they feel (wet, cold) and of the effect they have—rain makes puddles to splash in, snow is soft underfoot and can be held, unlike the rain. Take him out in the wind and discover what it does to a paper windmill, a balloon, the leaves off the tree, the clothes on the line. Make him aware of the warmth of the sunshine. Let him walk on low walls, on grass, pebbles; let him open and close gates, push the pushchair. Let him feel and smell the flowers.

These things are all around us and so familiar to us that we do not always realise that unless we take the trouble to draw the deaf/blind child's attention to them, he may never know about them. We do not overwhelm him by making him aware of all these things together—when we walk a certain way there may be a low wall to walk along, a slope to run down; another way we may find a gate to open and close, a gravel path to shuffle along—as these things become familiar, they help to identify the walk itself and make recognising them a reward.

Looking ahead

It would not be right to write a 'conclusion' to a programme of this nature—it is essentially a 'beginning'. You do not stop working with your child or expect him to go ahead on his own once he has progressed through and achieved the aims of the six stages. It is to be hoped that he is ready, and will have an opportunity of beginning, to mix with other preschool children and that you will be sharing the task of taking him on to the next milestones with the help of properly qualified teaching staff.

I hope the programme has enabled you to give your child a good start; also that it has enabled you to understand his needs and why the very special approach has been necessary. If you have been successful, you will realise the importance of continuing this approach, particularly as regards the method of communication (signing *and* speech), and the 'intervener' role of *all* who communicate with your child.

The ideas used in the programme have been gathered together over many years from the many remedial programmes which exist and from which I have taken those parts which successfully meet the needs of the deaf/blind child. Some were designed by well-known educationalists, others by classroom teachers and parents—to all of these people I, you and your child, owe much gratitude. They have covered the first set of milestones and I am sure you will have gathered that, while each prepared for the next, what resulted was not only improvement and refinement, but increase in breadth and depth. This must continue, and we must be very careful not to develop splinter skills—skills that are used only in one way and not integrated into new skills and used in a variety of ways. (Ideas for the next set of milestones can be found in my 1975 book *Understanding the Deaf/Blind Child.*) Generalisation must now be encouraged by enabling the child to do familiar things with different people, in different settings and at different times.

My best wishes go with you and your little one as you move into the future, and as I remind you of some of the more important points I have tried to emphasise throughout the programme.

1. You can help your child more than anyone else, but only if you accept help from others and take time off to relax and refresh yourself.

2. Your deaf/blind child is one of the family, not its centre.

3. A child learns best by doing, so do we, so ask the 'experts' to *tell* you what to do and observe you doing it rather than demonstrating.

4. The child must experience and understand an activity in detail before he can be expected to do it on his own. (So must we—see (3) above!)

5. When your child can do something on his own, let him. Remember sometimes to present the activity in a slightly different way so that there is a problem to solve—this way he learns to think and to apply his thinking when a similar problem occurs but in a different context.

6. Knowing what to do next keeps you one step ahead of your child. It is better to anticipate problems and thereby prevent them, rather than waiting until they exist and then having to treat them.

7. The deaf/blind child has to learn the same things as the seeing/hearing child—only the method of learning is different.

8. Observation of your child's behaviour provides the clues to his needs and proof of his abilities. Remember to base your observation on what the child *does*—you must not suggest a reason for this as it would be based on *your* own experiences which are unlikely to be those of the child.

9. If something outside the programme works better for you and your child, use it.

10. You are not alone in bringing up a deaf/blind child—there are many other families with a child who has the double disability. Much mutual help and comfort is to be gained by getting in touch with them through the National Assocation of Deaf/Blind and Rubella Handicapped (address in Appendix 4).

11. Like any other child, the deaf/blind one will have his off days—learning the way he does requires intensive concentration and this is tiring.

12. On those dark days (rare I hope) when you feel you are getting absolutely nowhere, ask yourself the following questions.

Am I quite sure I know exactly what it is I am trying to get over to my child?

Have I made the task simple enough?

Does what I do and the way I do it motivate the child?

Is there a reward in it for my child?

Have I given him enough information?

Have I made the steps small enough?

Have I made it fun?

Somewhere in your answers there will be the ray of light you need.

You may feel your child is unfortunate not to have the full use of his vision and hearing but, if you have been able to follow this programme, by now he will be lucky and have instead two pairs of hands, his own and yours.

Appendix 1

Schedules of normal development

On preparing these schedules I have made a careful study of the large number that exist today. Without the help of these, our understanding of the needs of the disabled child could never have advanced as quickly as it has. In preference to using any one of them by itself, I have listed those items which seem best to relate to the developmental stages to which we have to pay special attention when the child has a dual disability of deafness and blindness.

MOTOR DEVELOPMENT

Lifts head occasionally and only momentarily.
Pushes with feet.
Rotates head from side to side.
Grasps Mum's finger.
Rolls over from stomach to back.
Lifts arms in reciprocal situation.
Sits with support, slight head lag.
Raises head 90° without support.
Brings hands to midline.
Rotates head from side to side when prone.
Lifts head when on tummy.
Pushes against hard surface with feet.
Bears some weight on legs when held standing.
Can roll to side from back.
Anticipates pulling to sit by lifting his head.
Can turn head sideways and down.
When on tummy can support on arms.
Assumes crawling position—pulls knees forward but cannot lift tummy.
Sits without support momentarily.
When held upright, bounces.
When held upright can support whole weight briefly.
Can lean forward when sitting.
Raises himself to hands and knees in creeping position.
Can raise himself from prone to sitting.
Rolls from place to place.
Can keep balance sitting when turns head from side to side.

Can stand holding on to support.
Can sink to floor with bump.
Can sit self on chair.
Pulls self to standing position holding on to support.
Creeps on hands and knees.
Walks, both hands supported.
Toddles with one hand held, feet far apart, short steps.
Toddles alone unassisted.
Walks sideways holding on to support.
Stands alone, feet wide apart.
Walks upstairs with help.
Gets downstairs with bump method or comes down backwards.
Walks backwards.
Balance difficulties in turning round.
Walks more quickly, but not running.
Bends to pick things up without falling.

MANIPULATION

Grasp reflex.
Hands open—grasp reflex less.
Beginning to clasp and unclasp hands.
Holds a rattle placed in palm briefly.
Hands come together, plays with fingers.
Reaches for objects, but tends to overshoot.
Holds rattle or small object, grasps with palm; if drops cannot
    recover.
Shakes rattle.
Plays with own hands and fingers.
Two-handed approach to objects.
Can grasp objects, manipulates on table top.
Frequently lifts objects.
Takes objects to mouth.
Splashes in bath.
Extends arm for grasping.
May begin to show hand preference.
Grasps toes and feet.
Palmar grasp of cube—drops one cube when given another one.
Reaches objects with one hand.
Transfers an object from one to the other hand, retains small
    object when another is offered.
Feeds himself with biscuit.
Bangs cube on table.
Removes cloth put over his head.
Grasps palm and finger.
Tries to regain lost object by raking movement.
Reaches for nearby objects.
Releases against resisting surfaces.
Examines objects with hands as well as eyes.

123

Basal finger–thumb opposition to grasp.
Brings two cubes together for comparison.
Can pick up crumbs with pincer hold.
Index finger approach.
Can let go of things but not on demand.
Drops things intentionally.
Puts objects in and out of containers.
Interested in working movable parts of objects.
Purposefully moves toys from one place to another.
Simple formboards—forces pieces in.
Holds spoon with palmar grip.
Can turn pages of book.
Scribbles with crayon.
Reaches for distant objects.
Likes to play with small objects.
Explores objects of different textures.

SOCIAL EMOTIONAL DEVELOPMENT

Recognises familiar face.
Smiles spontaneously.
Increased affection and interest in family.
Shy with strangers.
Imitates gestures and facial expression.
Is pleased by own motor skills.
Can play alone for a little while.
Can play pat-a-cake, wave good-bye.
Varies behaviour according to reactions of others.
Shows fear, anger, affection, jealousy, anxiety, sympathy.
Begins to show a sense of humour.
Enjoys social contact and will imitate.
Imitates simple things he sees others do.
Enjoys being 'helpful'.
Cries if someone familiar goes away.
Resists change in routine.
Cries with irritation or frustration.
Goes through a period of resistance to authority.
Likes to mimic people.
Likes to carry around a familiar toy.
Plays alone.
Plays alongside other children.
Likes to hold on to own things.
More affectionate.
Shows pity, modesty, shame and guilt.
Imitates things present, not from memory.
May sulk.
Does not ask for help from adults.
Not interested in other children, treats as toys.
Likes dancing, clapping—gross motor activities.

Fears are mainly auditory.
Seeks help of adult.
Gets over temper tantrums more quickly.
Begins to share toys and take turns with other children.

VISUAL DEVELOPMENT

Stares at mother's face.
Follows object with eyes turning his head to midline of body.
Shuts eyes on stimulation with light.
Looks at object held 4″ above chest.
True ocular fixation.
Follows bright toy through 90°.
Follows moving person through 90°.
Shifts visual fixation by twitch-like movements of eyes.
Watches own hands.
Follows dangling toy through 180°.
Recognises feeding bottle on sight and makes welcoming movements.
Looks actively about.
Smiles at mirror image.
If toy dropped, follows it with eyes—if remains in visual field, will try to recover.
Recognises faces up to 6 yards away.
Watches TV picture from 3 yards.
Able to see tiny white objects lying near him.
Begins to be interested in pictures and books.
Uncovers object if sees hidden.
Anticipates whole object by seeing only a part.
Shifts visual attention from one object to another (scanning).
Visually seeks missing object or person.
Points with index finger.

DEVELOPMENT OF LISTENING

Startles at sound.
Ceases or increases activity when sound is introduced.
Responds to mother's voice.
Pays attention to tones in voices.
Turns to search for source of sound.
Discriminates between familiar environmental sounds.
Turns directly to source of sound.
Recognises own name and 'No'.
May notice difference between cross and friendly voices.
Enjoys music, particularly with good beat.
Can recognise simple commands one at a time.
Stops crying when hears familiar voice.
Understands 'Stop'.
Knows names of some body parts, familiar objects.

Enjoys nursery rhymes.
Remembers two-part command.

DEVELOPMENT OF VOCALISATION

Reflexive sounds.
Makes small throaty noises.
Different cries according to need.
Random sound making.
Coos and gurgles and laughs in response to others.
Copies his own sounds—babbles.
Indicates his wants by crying.
Produces high- and low-pitched sounds.
Imitates sounds of others.
Begins using specific sounds.
Can say single words.
Goes on to improve pronunciation.

DEVELOPMENT OF COMMUNICATION

Responds to gestures.
Uses voice to get attention.
Uses gestures; pulls and points.
Uses specific sounds to get specific response.
Puts adult's hand on object he wants help with.
Uses first words intentionally.
Seeks attention through noise making.
Plays at talking.
Uses jargon.
Uses up to 50 words.
Uses one-word sentence.
Uses two-word sentence.
Recognises pictures, cannot always name.
Talking accompanied with gesture.

TACTILE DEVELOPMENT

Enjoys being warm; dislikes rough textures and cold surfaces.
Enjoys body being massaged.
Responds to being touched, but cannot locate place touched.
Explores objects with fingers.
Can recognise objects without seeing.
Can indicate part of body touched.

DRESSING AND UNDRESSING

Does not participate at all.
Assists in dressing by holding up arm for sleeve.
Assists in dressing by holding out leg for sock or shoe.

Helps to pull off shoe, sock and hat.
Undresses with help.
Can pull down zips.
Can pull down pants.
Tries to put on own clothes.

NORMAL FEEDING DEVELOPMENT

Only small fluctuations in amount taken.
Sucking and swallowing reflexes.
Cries for food.
Sucking improves and associated activities involving mouth also
    appear.
Fusses for food.
Can drink from cup but ability inadequate.
Waits for food. Anticipates by opening mouth and closing lips
    round nipple. After feeding often sucks thumb and, if the
    sucking demand is strong, will interfere with solids.
Will drink fruit juice from cup. New foods can gradually be
    introduced.
Poor feeders still eat non-fluctuating amount of food.
Sucking decreased and solid food taken at each meal. Spoon
    feeding still maintained; is enjoyed. Head is orientated, mouth
    poised and food sucked from spoon.
Can adjust to mealtimes set by mother and shows preference for
    bottle or solids.
Will take juice from cup. Children often given more food than
    need—will eat rusk. Eats most of food given.
Co-ordination of tongue and pharynx sufficient to take purée.
    Munches rather than sucks if given rusk. Offers mouth as
    spoon approaches and swallows rapidly; has good lip
    approximation when drinking from cup—spilling occurs when
    cup taken from lip. Begins to hold bottle.
Vocalises in anticipation of food. Indicates preference by refusal
    of disliked foods.
Eagerness for food between 36 and 40 weeks.
Begins to be selective—type, temperature, one food or another—
    should not be expected to eat any particular kind and if choice
    is limited should not be concerned.
Holds cup and tilts head back to drain.
Enjoys finger feeding. May rub spilled food on tray and likes to
    hold spoon to brush across plate and put in mouth to lick. Likes
    to grab dish and spill.
Grasp of cup shows finger co-ordination. Drinks 5–6 swallows at
    a time. Finger action takes place of head tilting but too quick so
    spills. Bottle has been discarded.
Can sit through meal. Finger feeds well. Accepts being fed so long
    as is kept occupied. Wants to try spoon and will carry to mouth

what sticks to spoon which usually ends up upside down. Finds it difficult to fill spoon as it is dipped in food.

Appetite decreasing—preferences more positive. Appetite for milk from cup less.

Spoon held horizontally and elbow raised as spoon is lifted. Side of spoon put in mouth and spoon may be turned as enters mouth. May carry spoon from dish with fingers. Well-defined lateral chewing movements. Both hands used when holding cup—can finish whole glass.

Still finger feeds such things as peas. Takes what he cannot swallow from mouth. Feeds better if left alone. Likes special dish, spoon etc. Will give empty cup to Mum—automatically drops it if she is not there.

Spoon now inserted in mouth without using free hand in process. Has cut teeth so chewing easier and a rotary movement is used. Can hold small cup in one hand, can lift, drink from and set down. Can discriminate food from other objects and unwrap sweets.

Does better alone—partial feeding may improve appetite of some, others eat main dish better if given a spoonful of desert now and then. Poor eaters may need distracting by telling them stories. Is fussy about food. Will show he has had enough by holding food in mouth. Is prone to food fads.

Has fluctuating appetite—grades food into what he likes so well he feeds himself, that he likes well enough to be fed, and that he refuses absolutely.

Still goes on food fads and is ritualistic in demanding repetitions of food. Sequence of courses is maintained. Second half may need to be fed to him.

Likes puddings but they cannot be used as bribe. Good appetite—milk drunk quickly.

Wants foods that require chewing. Spoon held between thumb and index finger. Can use fork. Cup held well.

Eats well alone but apt to dawdle. Likes to help to choose food he will eat and to set table.

TOILETTING

Cries when wet.

No bladder control.

Begins to be dry for longer periods during day.

Shows interest in potty.

Sits briefly, but does not use potty.

May show control by using nappy after being on potty.

Uses potty occasionally.

Uses potty frequently.

Indicates needing to have bowel movement.

Accidents less frequently—may occur when upset, ill or excited.

Boys may begin to stand.

Integrated programmes

The following are some sample programmes which were designed individually for four young children with impairment to both vision and hearing who came with their parents to the National Association for Deaf/Blind and Rubella Handicapped Family Centre for help.

No two children are alike in age, degree or disability, family background and so on, but these programmes illustrate how various items can be brought together to provide a total approach which meets the changing and special needs of a particular child. The names are, of course, fictitious.

PROGRAMME 1

Vision

Katie (date of birth March 1981) 13.2.82
Katie has useful light and darkness vision and is able sometimes to fixate upon and follow briefly a source of light or reflection. We should encourage her to do this and help her to reach out and touch what she has seen. See if you can find out where she sees best, what she is most attracted to visually, and whether there is any colour which particularly takes her attention.

Communication

Respond to her attempts to 'tell' you something. Watch for movements which she repeats which you can help her to associate with something she likes, e.g. banging with her hand to be jogged up and down on your lap. Do this with her and then give her a chance to do it spontaneously—if she realises this is what gets her what she wants and she does it deliberately, she is communicating meaningfully and this is what we want to encourage.

Listening

Make interesting sounds which are associated with something happening to her, e.g. banging on the plate when her meal is ready for her to begin; making contrasting sounds with your voice. If possible, let her feel what makes the sound. If an instrument, encourage her to learn how to make the sound for herself. If she copies the sound you make with your voice (or tries), praise her for it; repeat it yourself and give her time to recognise the sound and organise her response. Remember the importance of sound and no sound at all—giving a good gap between sounds.

Hearing

Always talk to her. In routine situations use set phrases which have more emphasis on the word related to the activity. The activity must be one in which she is physically involved, for example:

> We are going *up* the stairs.
> Into your *bed*.
> Have some *more*.
> It's *all gone*.

When she is not wearing her hearing aids, speak close to her ear (do not shout, but speak clearly). Use good melodic intonation and, if anything, overdo the emotional content, e.g. express with the tone of your voice such feelings as fun, sympathy, praise, affection etc.

Tactile

Now that she is already happy to place her hands on your face, make sounds that will make her aware of the vibration or breath or lip shape—contrasting ones are more likely to be noticed—then put her hands on her own face. Put things in her hands and explore them with her, gently moving her hands over them, stopping to identify corners, texture changes and so on. Use objects which are connected with things that happen to her routinely. Let her feel your body and then her own.

PROGRAMME 2

Katie 24.7.82

In our first programme we were concerned to encourage Katie to use the vision and hearing she has (to learn to look and listen) and to progress towards sitting alone. She has made good progress in all three areas and you should continue along the same lines, noting the way she responds and extending her responses in new ways where you can.

We were encouraging her to learn about things by moving over them with her hands and exploring for the features that would help her learn to recognise them. Continue this and introduce a few contrasting objects—very soft and very hard, smooth and rough, cold and warm etc.—helping her to become aware of the difference. Try it yourself and you will find you touch something smooth in quite a different way from something rough, you quickly withdraw your hand from something very cold, but you linger when it is nice and warm—try to convey these differences to her through your reactions in your hands and body. Continue to make her aware of vibrations and rhythms—dancing with her in your arms or putting her hand on the radio when there is music with a good strong beat. Do not move too quickly, but make sure the tempo has emphasis.

Although Katie is still small physically, I think we can begin very gently to help her to learn about some of the things in her daily routines and round about her home that will enable her to recognise what is going to happen to her and where she is.

Let us look first at increasing Katie's awareness of what is going to

130

happen next. She has already begun to recognise that some things always follow each other, e.g. seeing the cup move across her vision means that she will have a drink, but this is an isolated situation and we have to build up for her what happens before the cup appears and what happens to it when she has finished with it. Very slowly, of course. Eventually, as simple experiences are widened, they begin to integrate with the other activities of which they are part—the milk is at mealtimes, milk plus cereal is the first of three meals and so on, until the day is full of meaning for her. Of course this takes a lot of time, but if you can begin to think of her training in this way, you will always know the next step ahead of her and be preparing yourself to teach it.

If we take bathing as an example, at this moment it involves being undressed, lifted into some water, being washed and dried, powdered and dressed again, but within each of these happenings there are things of which we need to make Katie aware by touch and movement to supplement the little she is getting from sight and hearing now. So, before going into the bath, help her to:

1. touch the bath,
2. 1.+feel the water with her hand,
3. touch the towel+2.+1.,
4. feel the soap+3.+2.+1.

This is just an example of how you build up a sequence; you can choose the things you feel go to make up a suitable one for you. It is important that there is something quite specific to define the beginning of an activity and the end. (This is particularly so of playing times. Within play activities there are also lots of opportunities to develop anticipation, not only of what comes next, but also of what I am expected to do next, which in turn leads to being able to do it oneself.) Increase the number of things that she can learn about the bathing situation very slowly—bearing in mind that very very much later on, what you are doing now will build up to knowing where the things for bathing are kept and to being able to gather them up before the bath and put them away afterwards.

In routines such as undressing and dressing, feeding, teaching how to play with toys etc.—all the things we expect children to do for themselves in time—we can make the best beginning by using the method which I described to you as the 'hands-on'. This way we ensure that the child is shown the best way to do things right from the start, and we give maximum help until we are certain that the child is absorbing the information and beginning to take over some parts of the activity. We do this because the poor information from vision and hearing often prevents the child doing this for himself and faulty information can lead to faulty behaviour. 'Hands on' means simply guiding the child through activities with you behind her and manipulating her hands with yours. This is best done to begin with with you sitting on the floor with Katie between your legs. While she is still small to work with in this position, it is a good time to start so that you develop the habit of teaching her this way and she gets used to learning from and through you. For example, you could now take her hands and move them down her leg before you take off her sock, and before you put it on move her hand up her leg. To put our socks on we have to bend forward and bring up our knee slightly—when you put her socks on from the co-active position your body movements will give her this information. The next stage would be to let her feel your hand pulling off the last bit of the sock and encourage her to try to do it on her own—and gradually you would encourage her to do the last two little bits, then the last three bits of taking off and so on until she can manage the whole operation. Children generally take things off before they learn to put them on. The technique with socks (and pants) is to hook the child's thumbs into the sides of the sock when showing them how to push off or pull on.

Recognising things that are special to a particular room in our home is how babies first learn about their homes—there's a place where I sleep, where I go in the bath, play with my toys, where Mummy cooks the dinner, Daddy keeps the car, and so on. They build up a kind of sensory 'map', and Katie will also have to do this by being made aware of smells, touch, knowing where the light source is, hearing and feeling the name given to the room through Mummy's voice or the sign if we have begun to use the appropriate one. If you can, guide her hand on to some of the more obvious things en route between one room and another (these are called reference points). For example:

1. helping you to push open the door as you leave a room and pulling open the one to the next room,
2. feeling the banisters when you are at the stairs,
3. bouncing upwards as you go upstairs and downwards as you come down,
4. make her aware through you of the changes en route—the step out of the front door or into the garden (if you have one).

I hope these ideas will set you thinking about others. Keep talking to her about what you are doing, what she is doing and what has resulted. In daily routines, continue to use phrases which give emphasis to the activity. Take things slowly and make sure that both of you enjoy what you do together.

PROGRAMME 3

Katie 16.10.82
Katie has made good progress since her last visit, particularly on the motor side which is so important to moving about to learn about the world around her. All the items on the last programme should be continued, but there are one or two more specific items you might now try.

132

First, anything you can do that will help her to learn to hold her head up and use her arms to bear weight will encourage her towards crawling—seek the advice of your physiotherapist on this. To encourage her to learn to 'feel' her feet and be more willing to put them to the ground, bounce her up and down or let her 'stand' without weight bearing on a variety of different surfaces, e.g. cotton wool, cork tiles, deep-pile carpet, lino. Use two at a time and make sure they contrast. You might try a warm surface and a cold one, a dry surface and a wet one—we want the sensitivity of the soles to be stimulated in this instance, hoping that it will motivate her to want to put her feet down and through this be preparing for the time when she is ready to walk. A lot of visually handicapped children dislike putting their feet on the floor to begin with, but soon get over it.

As we watched Katie playing on your lap we were able to identify movements she made to ask you to continue with a particular activity. This is her way of communicating with you. It is vital that you respond to her as she wishes, so that she learns she can ask for things herself. In time she will learn that different actions she makes get different results. There is a particular hand movement when she is thirsty and wants her milk, give her this signal (that is, take her hands and make the signal with her) before you give her the milk. When you judge that this is understood by her (and these things take time), you will link the normal sign for drink with *her* signal for drink and gradually fade out her signal, so that it gets replaced with the normal sign that is used. Watch for opportunities for other signals from her and use these in the same way. If there is a very positive action or game that you can do with her for which *you* can find a signal that somehow repeats a part of that activity, you can use that signal before you begin the activity. (Whirling round and round with her in your arms—if she likes it, this experience is a good one, the signal being waving the hand round and round.) After a while you will feel her recognition of the signal by movement in her hand under yours like the signal and you can then give her an opportunity to give you that signal when she wants you to continue the activity. This way communication is both from her to you and from you to her—the way all communication begins and grows.

As often as you can when you are speaking to Katie, put her hand over your mouth or on your throat. If you can get her to put her own hand on her mouth, throat or chest, when she is making sounds herself, do this.

In view of the fact that it is likely she has light and darkness vision, we should encourage her to look at things which we place, deliberately, between her and a light source. As she has also shown that she can follow the beam from a torch, you might try shining a light on a brightly coloured or light-reflecting toy and see if she can locate it. If she does pick up these visually, then show her how to reach for them. It might be worth organising a black matt background to enhance the brightness initially.

Katie needs to gain more control in the use of her hands, for these will be a major source of information for her. Play with her hands, touching the fingertips, tracing down the fingers to the palm, back and front, to increase her awareness of them. Show her how to pat things, bring the things she holds in her hands together—some that bang and some that do not make a sound. Develop the exploring which you were doing 'hands on', giving emphasis to the roundness of things.

Take the work with Katie slowly and if you feel tense, or she shows signs of tenseness, stop and do something you both enjoy and then call it a day . . . there is another day tomorrow.

PROGRAMME 1

Jane (date of birth 4.2.80) 21.11.82
Jane's behaviour indicates some good beginnings. She uses her vision to obtain things which are beyond her reach, to locate things she has dropped and to avoid objects in her way. Considering she has only been able to walk since June, her mobility is good and she was quick to adapt to the rooms in the centre using the light sources as her guide. She shows a listening attitude with her aids on and is making some pleasing sounds. She was not unhappy in a strange place and with strange people, showing interest in both. She has a good relationship with the members of her family and familiar people and the progress she has made at the nursery shows she is ready to learn. These are Jane's assets and what we are concerned to use and there are a number of things which can be done at home to help her learn about the world she lives in. These are things which we would naturally do with all children, but for Jane we need to do them in a more structured way.

First, Jane needs to be helped to become aware of (a) all the things that are used in daily routines, (b) the order in which they are used, and (c) what happens to them after they have been used. Let us take bath time as an example. The important things to get are her nightclothes, the towel, the soap and flannel and her bath toys—keep these in special places and let her help you gather them up and take them to the bathroom. When she is undressed let her feel the empty bath, the tap, then feel you turning it on (her hand over yours), feel the water coming out and going down into the bath. When she is in the bath, let her feel the flannel while it is dry, help you put it in the water and feel it again when it is wet. Then let her feel the soap, help you rub it on the flannel and then feel the flannel with the soap on it. Hold her hand on the flannel and show her how to rub it on her tummy. When she does not mind doing this (and I expect she will to begin with), you can add an arm, then both arms and so on, so that she is learning about the parts of her body. Let out the bath water but do not show her how to do this (yet) or she will do it for fun before you are ready. Let her sit in the bath until all the water is gone so that she knows she has to come out; it also provides you with a splendid opportunity to give the 'finished' sign. When she has been dried and dressed, let her help put the towel, soap and flannel in the correct places.

Our children need to know about *everything* that is going on, and since we cannot tell them and they may not be seeing in detail, they must share with us in *doing* things. If you can look at all the daily routine situations (e.g. getting up in the morning, mealtimes, going out for a walk, playtimes and so on) in the way I have illustrated above, Jane will gradually come to know what happens, to expect certain things to happen and eventually to be able to begin to do some parts for herself. Instead of the day being rather haphazard for her, it begins to have some meaning—it does not mean any change in your normal routine, only that you make the routines themselves ordered.

During each activity, *talk* to her about what you are doing in short sentences which have in them the name of the object or what you are doing with it, or maybe one of its characteristics. For instance, in bathing you could use:

Here's the *tap*.
Let's *turn* the tap on. } Before the bath.
Here comes the *water*.

Water *all gone*. } Before you lift her out of the bath.
Out you come.

Use the same phrases every time—write them down and keep them handy until it becomes habit to use them.

Once or twice a day, sit Jane on your lap with her back to you and say 'Now we are going to play', then do some nursery rhymes with actions with her (begin with one which you do several times and add to only gradually). Good ones are 'Pat-a-cake', 'This is the way the ladies ride' and 'The grand old Duke of York'. Sing the words to her and, with your hands over hers, show her how to do the actions. If she enjoys this, you will find she may make, or try to make, some of the movements herself and you must encourage this because imitation of movements is the basis of learning to sign to communicate. Do not expect Jane to make any sounds like your words (she has to hear these—if she is listening—for at least 6 to 12 months before she is likely to make any attempt to copy them), but listen out for any changes in the sounds she makes. Copy the sounds she makes and encourage her to play making sounds in turn with you.

Use the signs they are beginning at the nursery school, making sure they are given to her at exactly the same time as she is made aware of what they refer to, e.g. put her hand on her mouth just before the first spoonful of dinner reaches her mouth, give her the toilet sign just as she sits on the potty, and so on.

Help her to add to what may be incomplete visual information, that which she can learn by touch*ing*—show her how to move her hands round things that are round (balls, plates, saucepan lids etc.), how there are corners on square things, move her hands over rough things then smooth things so she can become aware of the difference, warm water and cold water, soft and hard things, wet and dry. It is by the contrast between opposites that she will first learn these things. Use her enjoyment of light to encourage her to play with things, e.g. playthings that reflect light, that she can *do* something with (other than spin). Always sit with her so that she has her back to you in order that you may guide her hands easily and that she may be using the correctly angled movements. Always tell her to *look* at things and, if she does not do this, gently turn her head in the right direction at the time you say the word 'Look'. It may help to raise your voice a little when talking to Jane just to get her attention.

If you feel that you can spend a few minutes regularly every day sitting at a table playing with Jane, the following ideas may be useful.

Have a box—a shoe box cut down to half its height is about right—into which you have put two objects which are exactly the same. (You begin with two and as Jane begins to be able to follow through the activity, then you can have three the same, four the same but not more than four; increase gradually.) You also have a small tray (the kind you get from the supermarket with meat in it) and you show Jane how to take one of the things out of the box, explore it and then put it on to the tray—then do the same with the other things in the box. Do not mix objects in the box (later on you can, but not at this stage) and use things like spoons, shoes, toothbrushes, things that are used frequently.

Make it lots of fun.

Praise her when she does a bit for herself.

Talk about the object and its features as she explores it with you.

Keep the session very short at first.

Do it only once per session for the first week or so, then do it twice or with two sets of objects.

Jane may not want to do this at first, but when she gets used to the idea that this is going to happen for a short while each day (preferably at the same time if possible), she will begin to tolerate it and stop protesting—eventually joining in because interest grows when resistance lessens. If you build up very gradually, she will not notice that the session is lengthening; what is important is that she is beginning to learn to sit for a short while and do something; this has to be taught before she will begin to play constructively of her own accord.

The principle of building up slowly applies to most things with children like Jane—feeding herself, toiletting, dressing herself and so on—and if it takes you a little longer to get things done now, both of you will benefit later on.

SPECIFIC COMMUNICATION PROGRAMME

John (date of birth February 1980) 8.4.83 (totally blind)
John has obviously made good and rapid progress during recent months and his listening and babbling skills suggest that he has some very useful hearing. Because it is felt that the use of signs sparked off the beginning of good sound making, I think it is important to continue to use signing alongside normal speech experiences until such time as we know for certain how well he is able to use his hearing.

The following ideas will provide a reminder and reference for the programme which we planned during your visit to the Family Centre.

1. Talk to John as you would to any child with normal hearing—but particularly about the things happening around him which have a sound he clearly listens to, e.g. the kettle boiling, the door bell etc.

2. Talk to him about *himself* and, when you do, give emphasis to the emotional tone in your voice, e.g. 'What a *good* boy you are', 'Are you a tired boy?', 'Who is a clever boy?'. He needs to have an awareness of feelings of people which we mostly express in our faces—he misses this, so we need to convey it through our voices. Here also, let him feel the vibration of your voice, by placing his hand either on your face or on your throat. Much of emotion is also conveyed to these children through our body—the way we hold them lovingly is different from when we are cross about something, and we need to remember this.

3. In situations which, because they occur regularly and frequently, are likely to be meaningful to John, use the following specific phrases, giving emphasis to the key words in them. The form of the sentences we discussed provides opportunities for John to make a response. For instance, if you say to him 'Here's your dinner', this does not need a response from him so the communication is only one sided. If, however, you say (and sign, of course) 'You want (some) dinner?', you can then take his hand and help him to sign ('I want (some) dinner, please'); this way he will learn that communication is a two-way process in which he can participate.

Mealtimes

Phrase: '*You* want (something) to eat?'
At the same time say the whole sentence, stressing the word 'you' and raising your voice to show it is a question.

Take his right hand and touch it to his chest (=you), then move it back towards you (=want), then back to his face touching his lips with fingertips (=eat).

You make the difference between the question and answer by making the pressure of his hand on his chest firmer (=I) and by the tone of your voice, which is now raised.

Now take his hand and *show him* how (using same signs) he can answer 'I want eat, please'.

Use this same procedure for drink, biscuit and more.

Remember, the word and sign must occur together or the association will not be made.

There are some instances when you are merely giving information and an answer is not required. 'All gone' is one, but I would not use this alone, I would sign 'Drink all gone' and 'Eat all gone'. Phrases like 'All gone' (and there are some others on the following pages) need to have a nice singsong sound to them. The reason is that children tend to notice the changes in pitch and repeat them for this quality initially rather than for their meaning. They may run them together and use them in the right places—John already shows an ability to imitate pitch changes and he should pick up these also. So listen carefully and see if he does make groups of sounds which resemble them—it is an indication of being able to remember a sequence of sounds and this is a very important skill in learning to speak.

'Wait' is a useful early sign, at mealtimes and in other routine situations. I would suggest that you say 'John, wait!' rather than 'Wait' on its own (pressing John's hand to his chest prior to giving the 'wait' sign).

Undressing and dressing

Here we have two aspects which we must be careful not to confuse.
    1. The name of the garment.
    2. The action you use to put it on and take it off.
Undressing. Touch his hand to the garment on him and *sign* its name, saying 'Take off your vest' (or whatever).
Dressing. Let him *feel* the texture and shape (or identifying features like the elastic in his pants); *sign* the name of the garment saying 'Put on your *pants*'.
Signing the whole sentence, i.e. 'Put on your pants', comes at a later stage when he has learned to recognise the sign for pants. Even later on, you can use the sentence 'Find your pants' and encourage him to answer 'Here they are', plus an extension from

you—'John put on his pants'—both helping to develop language and self-care.

Going to bed

Sign and say 'Time for bed' (touch his right hand to his left wrist, then put his hands together and up to the side of his head). You must do this just as he goes into his bed to begin with; if you say it anywhere else, he will not be able to make the association between bed and the word/sign. Give him some clues about bed also: take his hand and let him feel from the foot to the head of the bed so he gets the idea of it being a long, low thing. Make a big thing of the bump at the end of the bed which the pillow forms so that he learns to recognise this as the place where he gets in. If he is still in a cot, then let him feel the rails and the side going down for him to be put in.

Having a bath

Sign and say 'Time for bath' just before he goes in, at the same time letting him feel the water with his hand. With both bed and bath times *say* 'In you go' and 'Out you come' in singsong fashion, preferably with his hand on your face if you can manage this somehow.

Going out in the car

As you put on his coat and again as you go towards the car, take both his hands and make the 'car' sign (hands moving the steering wheel), at the same time saying 'brrr, brrr'.

Going out for a walk

As you put on his coat and again as you leave the house, make the 'walk' sign (walking movement of your index and middle finger down his wrist and on to his palm), saying 'Let's go for a walk' (singsong). Then take his hand and show him how to make the sign himself on his wrist and palm.

General comments

Whenever possible, encourage him to feel your face and lips when you are speaking to him (obviously not when you are signing with him). Imitate the sounds he makes; make it a game of taking turns, giving him plenty of time to organise his sound-making apparatus before you repeat yours. If the sounds he makes relate to a person or object (or seem to), give him the correct words so that he has an opportunity to hear these and gradually refine his sounds to match them. If possible, keep a written list of the words he tries to use. You already have the words 'down', 'ball', 'Daddy' and his own name. Whenever he does make an attempt to copy a word, praise him for it.

There will be many phrases which you will use automatically without realising it, and indeed you may find him trying to imitate some of these. If so, jolly good, and it is an indication that his deafness is not going to be such a serious disability. However, at the present time signing and saying specific phrases as I have outlined above, do provide John with the maximum opportunity for recognition, imitation and response. Because we are using them consciously, we shall give more emphasis to them and watch for his reactions. When we get a response in these situations, we can introduce others and expand the sentences in the normal way. And we shall, of course, come to know by the way he responds whether he is going to need to use signing permanently for communication.

PROGRAMME 1

Communication

Peter (date of birth April 1979) July 1983

I am sure you are wise to have decided that Peter should now use signing as his means of communication. It is vital that he waits no longer to develop communication skills if these are not to be limited in the future. It is always possible, providing he is always given a verbal input alongside the signing, that the ability to use speech may develop later. It is very important to learn to communicate—and by the means best suited to his present abilities.

Observing Peter's behaviour and listening to your comments about him, it is clear that he is making use of tactile information. This is splendid and a valuable back-up to his visual information. I would suggest therefore that, while expecting him to look at signs, learn to recognise and copy them visually, you also show him how to make these signs. This you do (from behind when possible) by guiding his hand(s) into the shape they must make, the position they take in relation to his body (close, touching, above the neckline etc.) and through the movement his hands must make (up, down, to the right/left etc.). If you can remember these three components of signing, it will help both you and Peter to remember the signs and make them more accurately. Having said that, of course, to begin with you must accept something that is very much less than perfect from Peter and respond so that he knows you have understood him—but always then show him the complete sign so that he is encouraged to improve his copy (this is what happens in normal language development).

Although we are showing Peter how to make signs, communication cannot be *taught*, it develops by being *used*. Signs, like words, have to be used, in context, a great many times before a child uses them spontaneously—a baby hears the word 'Mummy' thousands of times before he actually uses it with meaning, but he also practises making it long before this. It is therefore important that your choice of signing situations to begin with is related to something which Peter understands and which happens frequently and regularly, e.g. mealtimes, bathing, going to the preschool unit, dressing and undressing, and so on.

Because he has responded so well to the encouragement you have given him to develop an awareness of tactile information, I would recommend that you continue to do this. It in no way lessens his need to use his vision, but adds clues which enable a child to 'see' and remember things more quickly. Always 'demand' that he looks at things *and* at what he has to *do*, but, with your hands on his, encourage him to feel the object and show him the actions needed to achieve the activity he is engaged in. This is a recognised method—we call it 'hands on'—and it is better done from behind or to the side of the child so that he has correct and not mirrored directional information. (Your left hand is over his left hand, not over his right, as it would be if you were in front of him.)

Finally, remember that once Peter can do something for himself, do not do it for him. Independence is the most precious gift you have to offer him. Being able to do things for yourself grows from being allowed to—show him, help him, but all the time make a conscious effort to recognise even the smallest bit of an activity *he* can do, and gradually withdraw your guidance as his confidence grows.

Appendix 3   Book list

Brown, S. and Moersch, M. (1978). *Parents on the Team.* University of Michigan Press.

Buscaglia, L. (1975). *The Disabled and their Parents—a Counselling Challenge.* New Jersey: Charles B. Slack (6900 Grove Road, Thorofare, NJ 08086, USA).

Effron, M. (1975). *A Vision Guide.* South Atlantic Regional Centre for Deaf/Blind, Raleigh, N. Carolina, U.S.A.

Finnie, N. (1974). *Handling the Young Cerebral Palsy Child at Home.* London: Heinemann.

Fraiberg, S. (1977). *Insights from the Blind.* Human Horizon Series. London: Souvenir Press.

Freeman, P. (1975). *Understanding the Deaf/Blind Child.* London: Heinemann.

Hoey, A. M. (1977). *Listening and Learning.* Australia: Dominie Publishing.

Holle, B. (1976). *Motor Development in Children.* Copenhagen: Munksgaard.

Kaufman, B. N. *Son Rise.* New York: Warner Books (75 Rockefellar Plaza, NY 10019, USA).

McInnes, J. M. and Treffrey, J. A. (1982). *Deaf/Blind Infants and Children.* Toronto: University of Toronto Press.

Montagu, A. (1978). *Touching,* 2nd edn. London: Harper & Row.

Nolan, M. and Tucker, I. S. (1981). *The Hearing Impaired Child and the Family.* Human Horizon Series. London: Souvenir Press.

RNIB (1978). *Guidelines for Teachers and Parents of Visually Handicapped Children with Additional Handicaps.* London: RNIB.

Rostron, H. I. (1970). *Finger Play for Nursery Schools.* London: Pitman.

Scott, I. P. Jan, J. E. and Freeman, R. D. (1977). *Can't Your Child See?* Baltimore: University Park Press.

Sheridan, M. (1982). *Children's Developmental Progress from Birth to 5 Years,* 4th edn. Windsor: NFER, Nelson.

Sheridan, M. (1977). *Spontaneous Play in Early Childhood—Birth to 5 Years.* Windsor: NFER, Nelson.

Victoria Deaf/Blind and Rubella Association. (1978). *Happy Birthday, Antoinette.* Melbourne: Open Leaves Press.

Walsh, S. R., ed (1982). *Understanding and Educating the Deaf-Blind/Severely and Profoundly Handicapped, an International Perspective*. Illinois: Charles C Thomas.

Chaney, C. and Kephart, C. N. (1968). *Motoric Aids to Perceptual Training*. Charles E. Merrill, Columbus, Ohio.

There are not many books written about the deaf/blind, but there have been a great number of papers given at conferences and workshops in Britain and abroad. A bibliography of these can be obtained on application to the Librarian at the RNID, 105 Gower Street, London WC1E 6AV.

There are a number of newsletters and magazines concerned with or including information about the deaf/blind. Of these, the following are the most useful.

Information Exchange, RNIB, Education Department, 224 Great Portland Street, London W1N 6AA.

'*Newsletter*', National Association for Deaf/Blind and Rubella Handicapped.

Parents Voice, National Society for the Mentally Handicapped.

TALK, National Deaf Children's Society.

(For the addresses see the list of associations in Appendix 4.)

Appendix 4   Organisations which may help you

British Diabetic Association, 3–6 Alfred Place, London WC1E
7EE (01 636 7355)

Chest and Heart Association, Tavistock House North, Tavistock
Square, London WC1 9JE (01 387 3012)

College of Speech Therapists, Harold Porter House, 6 Lechmere
Road, London NW2 (01 459 8521)

DES (Department of Education and Science) Publications,
Government Buildings, Honeypot Lane, Stanmore, Middlesex

DHSS (Department of Health and Social Security) Publications,
Government Buildings, Honeypot Lane, Stanmore, Middlesex

Family Fund, Beverley House, Shipton Road, York YO3 6RB
(0904 29241)

Invalid Children's Aid Association, 126 Buckingham Palace
Road, London SW1W 9SB (01 730 9891)

Makaton Vocabulary Development Project, 31 Firwood Drive,
Camberley, Surrey

Mobility Allowance Unit, DHSS, Norcross, Blackpool, Lancs.

National Association for Deaf/Blind and Rubella Handicapped,
311 Gray's Inn Road, London WC1X 8PT (01 278 1000)

National Association for the Education of the Partially Sighted,
East Anglian School, Church Road, Gorleston-on-Sea, Great
Yarmouth, Norfolk (0493 62399)

National Children's Bureau, 8 Wakley Street, London EC1V
7QE (01 278 9441)

National Deaf Children's Society, 31 Gloucester Place, London
W1H 4EA (01 486 3251)

National Society for Mentally Handicapped, 117–123 Golden
Lane, London EC1Y 0RF (01 253 9433)

Pre-school Playgroups Association, Alford House, Aveline Street,
London SE11 5DJ (01 582 8871)

Royal National Institute for the Blind, 224 Great Portland Street,
London W1N 6AV (01 388 1266)

Royal National Institute for the Deaf, 105 Gower Street, London
WC1E 6AV (01 387 8033)

Voluntary Council for Handicapped Children, National Children's Bureau, 8 Wakley Street, London EC1V 7QE (01 278
9441)

Appendix 5

Toiletting chart

Time	M	T	W	T	F	S	S	M	T	W	T	F	S	S	M	T	W	T	F	*Comment*
7.45 a.m.																				
8.45																				
9.45																				
10.45																				
11.45																				
12.45 p.m.																				
1.45																				
2.45																				
3.45																				
4.45																				
5.45																				
6.45																				

The time given in column 1 represents an hourly check. So long as the check is at regular intervals, you make your own choice as to how often it is done.

The code for marking the square for each day is:

W = wet
D = dry
B = bowels open.

Where necessary you would use the combinations WB or DB.

Appendix 6 — An audiogram

When your child's hearing is tested the result will be described as a hearing loss of so many decibels (dBs). The chart below is to give you a very simple explanation of what this means. The child's responses to sounds (usually pure tone) fed into each ear separately are recorded on this chart. The loss is an average based on the age at which the impairment occurred and on the loss at frequencies 250 Hz to 4000 Hz shown for the ear with the smaller loss.

Frequency in Hz

Can hear	Loss	dBs	250	500	1000	1500	2000	3000	4000	6000
Birdsongs	None	10								
		20								
Whisper										
	Slight	30								
Normal		40								
speech	Mild	50								
		60								
	Moderate	70								
Lorry		80								
	Severe	90								
Drill		100								
Aircraft	Profound	110								

Frequency (Hz) describes the number of vibrations per second which make the sound. Frequency we describe as the 'pitch'— high and low—but this may sound different for each of us. Intensity (dBs) is the quantity of sound which we describe as loudness, but this also is a subjective judgement.

The dB loss is not a simple arithmetical progression—a 90-dB loss is much greater than three times the loss at 30 dB.

146

Huntercraft, Ransom Stable, Prestlands Lane, Sherborne, Dorset DT9 4EY
  Diffraction box
  Hexagons
  Windmill
  Zig-zag
  Fiddlesticks
Community Playthings, Robertsbridge, East Sussex TN32 5DR
  Rocking pony
Fisher-Price
  Rattles—various
  Turn-n-learn Activity Centre
  Rock-a-stack
  Bath Activity Centre
  Spinning butterfly
  Change a tune carousel
  Cassette recorder
Nottingham Educational Supplies Ltd, 17 Ludlow Hill Road, Melton Road, West Bridgford, Nottingham NG2 6HD
  Flip Fingers
  Wobbly Colours
  Maypole
Playaid Supplies, Shenval Estate, South Road, Temple Fields, Harlow, Essex CM2 O2BD
  Leybourne colour frames
  Nursery trampoline
  Rompa playball (various diameters)
  Pegboard weaving loom set
  Varilid posting box
E. J. Arnold Ltd, Parkside Lane, Densbury Road, Leeds LS11 5TD
  Active Baby Set
  Flying Acrobats
Abbatt Toys, Play Specials (As E. J. Arnold above)
  Translucent threading beads
  Colour hammer pegs
  Coloured patchwork balls
  Step-on-it

Duplo
   Rattles 2015, 2023, 2024
   Spinning rattle set 2037
   Bath activity toy 2038
   Rocker pull toy 2056
   Bumper pull toy 2053
   Building set 2370
Various
   Crazy Wheel
   Humpty Dumpty Flippo (sonic control) Winny Product
   Pegboards—preferably home made so that you can begin with
            2 holes only and have a series of boards with 4, 8,
            12 and 16 holes
   Bicycle bell or horn
   Three-colour torch
   Disco mat (use above or below play rug)
   Fan torch (lights up one end/blows other—H. A. L. Rowe Ltd)
   Set of activity bricks
   Transparent ball with spinning centre
   A slinki
   Spinning tops—large press down
   Spin rattle (suction base with rattle/mobile at top)
   Jolly Wobbler Rattle (suction base with rattle/mobile at top)
   Large snap lock beads
   Jumping penguin (wind up)
   Flip finger rattle
   Dumbell rattles
   Click-a-wheel (two-handed rattle)
   Popup Cone Tree
   Jack in a box—push-button type and turn-handle one
   Musical Redbird (hangs up—pull on string to make it sing)
   Penguin Clicker (dial and it clicks)
   Jerry Giraffe (wind up)
   Turn Turtle (wind up)
   Clic-Clac rattle
   Brio threader
   Peek-a-boo bunny—pull string to play music

Appendix 8 Finger Spelling. The deaf-blind manual alphabet

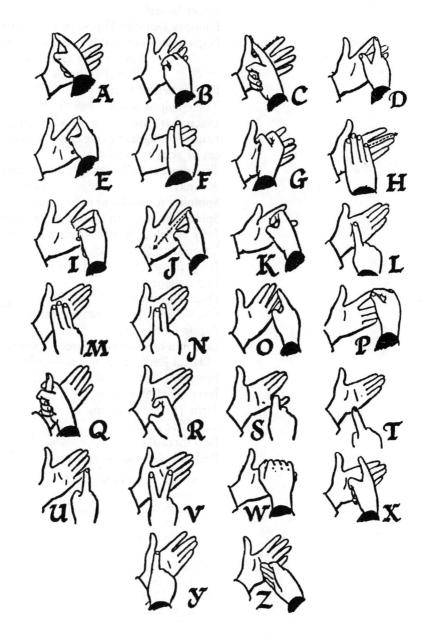